A WORKING FAITH
FOR THE WORLD

A
WORKING FAITH
FOR THE WORLD

by

HUGH VERNON WHITE

Secretary, The American Board of
Commissioners for Foreign Missions

ΛΑΜΠΑΔΙΑ ΕΧΟΝΤΕΣ ΔΙΑΔΩΣΟΥΣΙΝ ΑΛΛΗΛΟΙΣ

HARPER & BROTHERS PUBLISHERS

New York and London

1938

To

JOHN WRIGHT BUCKHAM

CONTENTS

Foreword

THIS BOOK UNDERTAKES AN AMBITIOUS TASK AND NO ONE CAN BE more conscious of its imperfections and insufficiency than the author. The excuse for writing it is that even the ordinary citizen today is forced to decide, either positively or passively, issues of the widest outreach and consequence. What is the true nature of man? What is the true bond of social solidarity? Can man govern himself, or must he have a master? Once more the lines of religious faith and political theory converge—at the point of man's conception of himself and his place in the universe. Today we must have a faith and a conception of life to guide and undergird us. No failures of historic Christianity, and they have been many, should hide from us the fact that the Christian faith holds the true answer to our need.

But such an affirmation requires that we make clear what is Christian and what is not Christian. I have tried to do this at some of the most vital points. In doing so I have made use of a term now somewhat in disrepute—liberal Christianity— to designate the true Christian faith. I have tried to make clear what liberal Christianity is and what it is not. Nothing is more necessary or would be more significant today than the full flowering of an evangelical Christianity in the atmosphere and conditions of the modern world, and that is what I mean by liberal Christianity.

Roman Catholic Christianity made its historic contribution; so did Protestantism. But they were stages along the way. Revolutions in thought and in social, industrial, economic and political life have revealed intrinsic limitations in those historic forms. They become increasingly irrelevant and obstructive to the original purpose of Christianity. The living Spirit calls for new and truer expression; the plight of the world cries out for an answer Christianity can give. But it must be a Christianity that can speak the language and work at the real tasks of the present day. It must be, no less, a Christianity vividly aware of its own essential truth and purpose, and moved by a prophetic passion for its historic mission. What has recently been known as liberalism has often lacked this depth of faith and its trend has been toward an impotent secularism. But the springs of power are in that faith, for it is faith in God and dedication to His work begun by Christ. In method liberalism has been right; its language has been that of the real world. Now it needs a return to God, to true religious faith; it needs to leave the reformer's egotism and truculence or sentimentality for the prophet's passion. A Christianity thus renewed calls for followers and claims allegiance of the peoples of the world.

Every Christian today should face these issues of a working faith. The purpose of this book is to focus attention upon them and to do something toward making clear the course the Christian Church should follow. I am greatly indebted to colleagues in the American Board, and to many others who have taught me and put me into touch with sources of information, and who have helped me to think things through. But full responsibility for all the book contains is mine. It represents my own thought and earnest conviction and, of course, my limitations of knowledge and outlook in many matters too great for me.

HUGH VERNON WHITE

Brookline, Mass.

PART I

Christianity a World Faith

CHAPTER I

The World's Need of a Unifying Faith

ANY RELIGION OR PHILOSOPHY WHICH PROFESSES TO HAVE A FUNDA-
mental answer to the problem of human life faces an unusual
situation of opportunity and testing today. The prevalence of
confusion and violent change throughout the world may easily
obscure the demand of the human spirit for a working faith,
but there are abundant signs that mankind is seeking a security
of life which is not merely social and economic but spiritual
as well. The very passion of the peoples, as they follow national
programs and range themselves behind the banners of the
fascist and communist ideologies, reveals a desperate quest for
a truth that can be whole-heartedly believed, and a cause to
which men can give themselves in soul and body. It is a period
of passionate and uncritical thinking and intemperate partisan-
ship. Even in our own country, which is relatively peaceful
and where, in the main, the orderly processes of life still go
on, we are constantly charging each other with being embodi-
ments of those evil spirits whose gigantic shadows stretch
across the world.

In the midst of this stress and excitement a Christian movement that is now geographically a world movement goes on.
Christianity is in the world; it is aware of the kind of a world
we are in today; it is bringing to full and free expression some
of the truths and principles for lack of which the world suffers
—truths and principles which have too long been made impotent in organized religion but which are the answer of
original Christianity to the spiritual quest of man. Man is on a

spiritual pilgrimage and Christianity has a clear and true word to say regarding the end of his journey and the spirit that can guide him successfully to the goal.

One can go to almost any country today and find men either feeling their way to new orientations of social, economic and intellectual life, or fanatically defending new forms that have not yet become firmly established. Perhaps the most significant and dramatic center of vast change just now is China, not alone because of her struggle with Japan, nor mainly so, but because, after resisting the idea of change for more than a century while the West beat upon her doors and edged itself into her domain, China has finally put her own mind upon the matter and taken into her own hands the forging of a new national life. If we would get at the heart of world change we cannot do better than to study the inner aspect of China's vast undertaking.

In October, 1935, I attended the Rotary Club meeting in Peiping. The speaker of the day was Y. S. Djang, professor of history in Tsing Hua College, the college founded by Boxer indemnity money returned to China by the United States. Professor Djang spoke on "My Year in Europe." He had spent four months each in Russia, Germany and England. His report of conditions in these three countries had to do particularly with liberty of thought and speech, industrial efficiency, and the degree of assurance the people had in their way of life.

In spite of improvement in recent years he found Russia very backward in the efficiency of her factories. He lamented the suppression or expulsion of non-conforming intellectuals, especially those in the field of history. Everywhere people eagerly asked him what he thought of Russia's achievements.

In Germany there was high technical efficiency, but no more intellectual freedom than in Russia. Germans, also, sought his good opinion of what their Nazi State was doing. When the Chinese traveler got to England he found factories operating upon a high level of productivity, and complete freedom of thought and utterance. From the Hyde Park orator to the university he found Englishmen thinking and expressing their minds freely on every conceivable subject. He could go where he pleased and see everything that was going on, but nobody ever asked him what he thought about the wonderful works of Britain or seemed to care a hang what he thought.

Professor Djang summed up his final impression as follows: "When I left China a year ago I was of the opinion that we in China need a dictator. China is so confused and disunited that she needs a strong government and it seemed to me that only some form of dictatorship could supply it. But having studied dictatorships in two countries and liberalism in another, I have come home with the profound conviction that China must work out her destiny upon the basis of a liberal order."

In Tientsin I asked Professor P. C. Chang of Nankai University what objective the government had in view in its rapidly developing educational system. He replied, "We cannot tell yet what our educational objective is, because we do not know yet what our social-economic order will be. It is certain that we shall not merely copy western capitalism, especially now that capitalism is showing such radical weaknesses in the very countries where it is most highly developed. Nor shall we take over communism as it is being worked out in Russia. We shall learn from both capitalism and communism, but we cannot tell yet what the ultimate form of our economic society will be. Since education should prepare people to understand and live in society, we must know the form and ideals of our society before we can define the objectives of our education."

As this is being written it seems doubtful whether China is to be free to work out her national destiny according to her own ideas, but nevertheless these statements by two of China's thoughtful leaders are significant of a world-wide crisis of peoples striving to bring to clear expression a satisfying ideal of national life and destiny. This is a matter not alone of economics, nor even of education, but of the spiritual meaning of life as well.

The chief symptom of this spiritual travail is the prevalence of one-party government in many countries. In Russia, it is the Communist party that controls the Soviet and yet the communists number only a small percentage of the population. It is theoretically possible for some other party, with other economic and cultural objectives, to control the Soviet system. In China there is, constitutionally, a republic, but the actual power is completely in the hands of the Kuomintang. Italy, formally, is a monarchy, but so absolute is the rule of the Fascists under Il Duce that the world has all but forgotten King Immanuel. Germany has still the structure of a republic but it is Nazi rule that uses at its will all the agencies and instruments of government. In Turkey the People's Party manipulates a theoretically representative republic and tolerates no opposition party.

In soviet, republic, and monarchy, whatever the official form of government, it is the Party that really governs. There is nothing in the political structure of any of these countries to explain this fact. Some other party, if it were strong enough, could use the same governmental machinery for its own ends, or really representative rule might exist with different parties seeking power through free elections.

There are various special reasons for the rise of one-party government in each of these countries—the stress of economic confusion, the breakdown of incipient democracy, or the fear of enemies. The one clear moral to be drawn therefrom, however, is that the form and constitution of the political state do not define the national objective nor furnish a basic philosophy for national life. Every nation must have such an ideal to give meaning and value to existence. The rise to power of the Party is due not to any new political idea but to its advocacy of a positive conception of the nation as a spiritual whole with certain values that are worth living and dying for. That this conception is hazy and unimpressive to the alien does not matter. Ultimate ideals are always only vaguely de-fined. Their power lies in the fact that they affirm the worth of the nation and call the individual to share in its power and glory.

The one-party system, whatever its actual course in any country today, vividly and even violently expresses the need which mankind has for a positive faith to which the whole man may be devoted, heart, intellect, and will. Such a faith is not merely an academic philosophy nor an abstract science. Academic thought is despised in such a time as this, and as for science, its methods and results are subordinated to the national program and its ethic of impartial truth is scorned.

The national obsessions that are being fostered today have much more the quality of religion than of science or phi-losophy. They do in fact fill the role of religion. They show dramatically that men need and will have a religion. We have been so much concerned over the attacks upon organized

Christianity in Germany and in other countries that we have overlooked the tremendous assertion in these party programs of man's basic need for a religious faith. To knit a people together in significant unity and to give the individual a spiritual home and a sense of value there must be a faith which is shared by all and which reaches to the roots of thought and feeling. This is the role of religion, and the quest of the nations today offers a direct challenge to Christianity. A true and vital Christianity has the answer to this challenge.

The Church once furnished a living, unifying faith for Christendom, but for three centuries now the Western world has been progressively secularizing its life. Education, art, philosophy, social life and politics have declared their independence of religious control. Even morality has become largely secular. All this is obvious and has often been said in recent times; but now we face a paradoxical situation and one that may mean a reversal of the policy of spiritual fragmentation. The paradox is this: men have rejected religion because of its restraints upon freedom; now they are almost joyously throwing away freedom for the sake of a pathetic substitute for religion.

For this development the prevailing form of religion itself has been largely responsible. The Church did by its dogmatic rule oppress the spirit of man. The principle of its control of human life was oriented to a future world and dominated by a doctrine which made that rule irrelevant to, or contradictory of, the real needs of men. The simple humanism of the gospels was blighted by the radical other-worldliness of the Church.

Protestantism made no real improvement over the Catholic system in this; indeed, in some ways it represented a backward step. The Lutheran churches surrendered the secular life to the state and centered their interest in a sphere called spiritual where salvation was to be found by the special, revealed techniques of faith. This course really laid the foundation for the secular nationalism of today, and even gave divine sanction to that nationalism by making the Church a state church and thus subservient to the national interest. Even those who most deeply sympathize with the Church in Germany today and most admire it for its courage in resisting the claims of the Nazi State must see that the Church itself has had its own share of responsibility for the present exaltation of the secular state as absolute. The denouement of modern history in Germany reveals the complete fallacy of a radical separation of the organized and professed religion of a country from its general human concerns. It is pertinent to note that the present struggle between Church and State in Germany is based, not upon ethical, but upon ecclesiastical grounds. That is, the Church is not opposing the State or being opposed by the State because the Church is standing, in the name of God, for a Christian ethics in the common life. It is not social or political righteousness for which the Church is making its heroic struggle, but freedom in the realm of religious education and Church government. Even in these matters the universalism of Christianity is in opposition to the national particularism of the National Socialist philosophy, but it remains true that the cause of conflict is theological and not ethical. The Church is suffering, not because it has demanded the embodiment of Christian ideals in the common life of Germany, but because it resists the totalitarian State with its claims of ecclesiastical autonomy based upon its own doctrine of divine revelation.

The Calvinist churches did take seriously the task of ordering practical life according to religious principles. The result was a theocratic state. Geneva, Scotland, and New England were scenes of this attempt to bring human life under the rule of God. Great moral and social benefits have accrued from it. There were evils also which derived from this conception and those evils have perhaps been magnified in recent years. But the fundamental fallacy of the Calvinist method was its conception of the divine control as legalistic. Old Testament legalism instead of New Testament grace was the basis for the Calvinist theocracy. Since the New Testament scriptures do not contain codified laws the Calvinist churches went to the Old Testament, which does have such codes, and took both specific commandments and the legalistic principle therefrom.

Here was discipline and authority but not freedom for the human spirit. Even apart from the biblical criticism that removed the basis of formal authority upon which the theocracy rests, the demand for intellectual and spiritual freedom was bound to destroy or push aside the religious control that it exercised. The result of the failure of theocracy has been a secular development in all areas of culture and morals. In our own country the separation of Church and State, designed to insure religious liberty and to free politics from ecclesiastical control, has contributed to the development of a national life devoid of any deep and worthy bond of spiritual unity.

Now that the world situation has shown so plainly that nations need a bond of unity and a faith that gives dignity to human life, a new demand is laid upon Christianity to meet this need. For that need can be met only by a religion, and Christianity is a religion and a religion-centered way of life. The national ideologies are bound to pass away. They are muscle-bound by their narrow outlook and, in a world where all today must deal with each other, they operate only to destroy each other. They are patently false and adventitious. They solve no human problem; they have no deep and true insight into human nature; they are philosophies of hate and war and furnish no true basis for human unity. The nations must turn in the end to an authentic religion and find unity in a really profound conception of man and his place in the universe. The answer to present world turmoil is a new Christendom, a world unified by the faith and ideal of a new Christianity. In view of the failure of old forms, however, it is clear that it must be a Christianity freed from the dogmatic metaphysics of the Catholic Church, and from both the irresponsible other-worldliness of Lutheranism and the legalistic conception of Calvinism. It must be a Christianity which recognizes the will of God as supreme over all life, individual and national, and which accepts the task of translating the will of God as clearly expressed in the New Testament into terms of personal morality and social, economic, and political laws and institutions. This kind of Christianity and this alone can furnish the world with a faith that will glorify life and that will give both the individual and the nation a noble calling. This faith will be firmly grounded on a metaphysic of Christian theism; and it will have an ethic of Christian love. These two elements naturally go together; either without the other is impotent and languishes in a world of skepticism and selfishness.

Such a faith Protestantism is finally beginning to formulate. It is to be fervently hoped that liberal Protestantism will move positively, consciously, and courageously in this direction. Even the more conservative Protestant churches have turned in varying degree to such an interpretation of Christianity. And the recent revival of theism in the liberal wing of Protestantism gives hope that the enervating skepticism which has deprived the liberal zeal for a Christian ethic of spiritual power will be replaced by a positive faith adequate to explain and support that ethic. The course taken by the Catholic Church offers no hope for the future, nor is there any likelihood that the Catholic Church will change its ways sufficiently to give it real spiritual significance in the new world with its social, economic and intellectual demands. Lutheran Christianity, despite its heroic stand in Germany, has no working faith and philosophy for this present world. The survival of Calvinism in fundamentalist Protestantism and its revival in Barthianism are both intellectually and ethically irrelevant to the needs of the world of today and tomorrow. If Christianity is to be the living faith of the future it must be a Christianity shorn of the limitations that have bound these historic movements, and committed to the basic theology and ethics that are truly Christian.

Christianity has both a theology and an anthropology; both a doctrine of God and a doctrine of man. It holds the will of God supreme; it finds its key to the knowledge of God's will in the spirit and precepts of Jesus and in his life; it takes as the historic task of the Church the transformation of humanity from center to circumference, by the power of God, into the Kingdom of Heaven. It believes in man as made in the image of God and capable of real redemption. It trusts in the grace of God as able both to save individuals from selfishness and sin and to create among men and nations a true community. Protagonists of Christianity so conceived—and as such truly conceived—have no illusions about the tragic evils of human life. We have had to bring this faith to the test of both the inner weaknesses of individuals and the gigantic sins of class and nation. It takes a stout heart to hold such a faith in the present world. But this faith is true! What else can one follow? It tells the truth about God. It tells the truth about man. The decades may be against it; the centuries are with it. To surrender it is to give over humanity to endless and hopeless strife. This is the faith of Jesus; it is the meaning of Christ in history. It is the only faith that gives history itself any hope or promise.

One historic product of Christianity that has been generally accepted and incorporated into the national programs and philosophies of the day is a certain humanitarianism, a professed concern for the welfare of man. Despite its other-worldliness Christianity has contributed powerfully to the creation of this sense of human worth. Back of all its formal theologies has been always the great truth that God cares for man. Nobody else may care much for him, but the common man has a secure ground for his worth and dignity in the love of God. This is his ultimate moral defense against all oppression and wrong, against all debasement and contempt at the hands of more powerful men. In its extremity the soul of man makes its appeal, past all human powers and institutions, to God.

This religious doctrine has made possible a true conception of personality. No naturalistic doctrine can produce an idea of man that makes him worthy of high respect or that lays upon him the moral necessity for high achievement. Nor can rationalism create such a conception. Rationalism may conceive man as an intelligence. But an intelligence, while it is a knower, is not intrinsically a doer and much less a lover. Nor would one be stirred to heroic service on behalf of a society of rational intelligences. One might admire them and wonder at them; one would hardly love them. There is much less glory for God than some suppose in a modern physicist's tribute that God is like a great mathematician. There is nothing intrinsically great or spiritual, certainly nothing to worship or adore, even in a heavenly mathematician. A mathematician may be lovable but it will be because he is a *man*, not because he is a mathematician.

The most dogmatic form of humanitarianism today is communism. It is doubtful if communism could or would have come into being had it not inherited this Christian valuation of man. Communism may not unjustly be called a Christian heresy because it has perverted an essentially Christian article of faith. Man derives his greatness from a being greater than himself—from God—and he cannot claim that greatness through submission to an economic society which has no transhuman reference save to the subhuman nature from which comes his physical existence and sustenance.

During the modern period of Christian missions Christianity has disseminated widely its concern for man. The role of Christian missions in world affairs cannot be fully understood unless we realize that any great religion carries with it forms and ideas which modify profoundly the culture of any country to which it goes. This is quite apparent in regard to Islam, which is a true "totalitarian" religion in that it provides legal, moral, artistic, and political forms for human life, as well as more strictly religious beliefs and practices. It is also true of Buddhism. When Buddhism spread in China and Japan it took with it a high speculative philosophy and an artistic impulse and influence. As a result, much of the philosophy and art of these two countries is Buddhist.

So, apart from any arbitrary transfer of superficial forms in manners and morals, which has justly been called cultural imperialism, Christianity always carries with it certain ethical and cultural values. This cultural embodiment in the modern period of expansion has not been primarily an ecclesiastical order—at least in respect to Protestant missions—but the main elements of Western civilization, especially those elements most expressive of the Christian faith itself. Chief among these are: (1) scientific technique of life in medicine, sanitation, and basic conveniences; (2) the ideal of general education; and (3) the humanitarianism that grows out of the Christian conception of personality.

These elements are not superficial aspects of culture. It is true that they are not exclusively Christian; but they are natural fruits of the Christian view of the world and man, even though some of them appear late in the history of Christian civilization. The progress of Christianity in the modern period has been greatly facilitated by the fact that the missionary has been a devoted and indefatigable agent for the communication of these values to the world at large.

Today, however, all round the world, science, education, and even humanitarianism are being cut loose from their Christian origins. But they will not and cannot stand on their own feet. They are not autonomous enterprises. They derive from deeper sources. Today they must attach themselves to some dominant philosophy of life, or be dragooned into service of some dominant power. A man high in American diplomatic circles in China pointed out to me that no government today can afford to let any other agency get credit for such basic services to the people as those of health and education.

Science, education, medicine, will not remain free and independent; indeed, they have already been made servants of Nationalism. And even humanitarianism is being claimed by the dominant State. Nationalism is promising welfare to the people. The parties that rule have taken names to represent this. In Turkey it is the "People's Party," one of whose six principles now written into the constitution is "popularism." "Communism" and "National Socialism" in Russia and Germany convey the same suggestion, and the Kuomintang in China, being interpreted, is simply the People's Party. There is no reason to doubt the sincerity of the leaders in these countries, but there is every reason for examining critically their conception of the man whose welfare they seek and claim to serve, and also the methods they propose to use. The question is, do they have a true anthropology? In this field Christianity claims to speak with authority. In so far as the idea of man which underlies or is embraced within these systems is contrary to the Christian idea, it must be looked upon as inadequate and bound to issue not in real human welfare but in human loss and degradation. A high doctrine of man is not easily attained or held. It is not an achievement of natural science. It requires religious faith to acquire it and religious passion to sustain it, both in theory and practice. Christianity cannot look with unconcern upon these secular claims to care for man. It must urge the larger conception and seek to win to it the people and eventually the governments of the world. It must evangelize the doctrine of man in every national culture.

The Christian faith which will undergird the life of men and nations and furnish a spiritual bond of unity for the world must have a metaphysic in which men really believe. The doctrine of man that is needed to support a true humanitarianism must be grounded in a doctrine of God. No absolute value for man can be derived from natural or human sources. The actuality of man and the evolutionary history of man alike fail to invest him with any sacredness that demands the respect of his fellows or even of his own mind. A navigator must find his position and direct his course by reference to the sun or the north star. Even the accurate surveying and measuring of the earth requires a celestial reference. Likewise, in any true estimate of man he must be viewed in relation to God. Man must discover his direction and plot his course, even in this mundane existence, by a heavenly fixed reference. God is of necessity the spiritual first principle of truly human living.

The achievement of faith in God is never wholly a matter of intellectual effort. The heart and will have their urgency and lay upon reason its duty to interpret their testimony and furnish life as a whole with a cogent conviction. But the intellectual task cannot be shirked. Christianity has no secure ground upon which to challenge either the ruthless inhumanities or the specious humanities of secular faiths unless it believes rationally as well as emotionally that God is, and that the supreme end of man is to worship God and do His will. No new economics or sociology, no crusade for Christian social ideals will have much significance unless it is firmly rooted in a belief held to be true of the sovereign and holy God. Ethical Christianity is an unstable sentiment apart from such a belief; based upon such a faith it becomes God's specific activity in human history.

Fortunately successive onslaughts of intellectual secularism have failed to do any real damage to the faith of religion. Religion *is* faith, not demonstrated knowledge as both Catholic and Protestant orthodoxy have affirmed. But as faith it is not only rational but vastly more rational and adequate to all the facts of life and the nature of man than any naturalistic doctrine. Religious faith is finding itself and gaining new confidence in the world of scientific and philosophical thought. The competent theologian today shows a maturity of thought and an inclusiveness of view sometimes lacking in other intellectual circles. It is a time for men of faith to undertake with even greater seriousness the structural task of theology. The theologian will furnish the faith of the world with its solid intellectual conviction, or that faith will not have power to gain the world and do its work of unity and peace.

When we assert, therefore, that Christianity has the unifying faith and objective for human life, we must face the full import of this demand for the conviction of *truth* about God as the antecedent of a Christian conception of man and as the support of all enterprises of Christian social idealism.

There are also certain minimum requirements of method if the Christian faith is to become established and if it is to operate effectively to produce its characteristic fruit. Freedom of the spirit and liberty of thought upon the vital issues of human life must be claimed as indispensable to it. The institution of religion has itself been too often the obstacle to free inquiry. It has persistently identified positive faith with closed dogma. One service secularism has done for spiritual progress has been its successful challenge to this ecclesiastical suppression of intellectual liberty.

Today the threat to freedom of thought comes not from religious but from secular sources. President Conant, at the Harvard Tercentenary celebration in 1936, pointed out this change. He said:

For the development of a national culture based on a study of the past, one condition is essential. This is absolute freedom of discussion, absolutely unmolested inquiry. We must have a spirit of tolerance which allows the expression of all opinions however heretical they may appear. Since the seventeenth century this has been achieved in the realm of religion. It is no longer possible for some bigoted Protestant to object if any person within the universities or without expounds sympathetically the philosophy of St. Thomas Aquinas. It is no longer possible for a member of the Roman Catholic Church to take offense at a critical discussion of Galileo's trial. Statements believed to be erroneous are met openly and fairly by counter arguments. But there is no persecution; there has been an end to religious bigotry in this country, and there are no signs of its return.

Will the same conditions prevail in the future when political and economic problems are examined? Unfortunately there are ominous signs that a new form of bigotry may arise. This is most serious, for we cannot develop the unifying educational forces we so sorely need unless all matters may be openly discussed. The origin of the Constitution, for example, the functioning of the three branches of the Federal Government, the forces of modern capitalism, must be dissected as fearlessly as the geologist examines the origin of the rocks. On this point there can be no compromise; we are either afraid of heresy or we are not. If we are afraid, there will be no adequate discussion of the genesis of our national life; the door will be shut to the development of a culture which will satisfy our needs.[1]

It is in the fields of history and economics that free investigation and the pursuit and expression of truth are most con-

[1] *Notes on the Tercentenary,* Harvard University Press, pp. 68, 69.

sistently denied. It is significant that in the mission schools and colleges of most countries today history must be taught by nationals. No foreigner is permitted to do that job. There is too much mythology mixed with the facts of history. Totalitarian states determine what is truth in all fields where teaching has any bearing upon national policy. This imposition of mental bondage surpasses anything an autocratic Church ever did to interfere with the free search for truth.

The faith for the future requires free history, free science, free philosophy, and free religion. Christianity demands such freedom; in the name of truth and of God it claims for man the right and duty to find the truth in every field and to bring to bear upon human conduct the natural influence of truth.

Particularly does Christianity call for full religious freedom. In varying degrees that freedom is limited or denied in many countries today. In Japan a secularized Shinto still demands of every subject supreme loyalty—above religion—to the emperor, that is, to the State. Turkey grants freedom of religious faith and worship but puts the ban on public teaching of religion, even in private schools. The unequal law in Russia guarantees freedom of religious confession (not teaching) and of anti-religious propaganda. All these forms of repression are imposed in the interest of national unity and the supremacy of political authority. They can be understood and even in some degree sympathized with in the light of past events and present national programs. But such denial of religious freedom, of the freedom to worship and to teach, destroys a basic condition for the realization of any sound national faith. It is a policy of fear and distrust. No national doctrine built upon such a foundation can be secure. It is bound to be destructive of the finer things within the nation and a menace to just and cordial relations with other peoples.

So far as method is concerned Christianity must ultimately trust to both intellectual and religious freedom. The person of Christ does not need to be shielded from investigation and comparison. The Christian doctrine will not suffer from free critical examination. It can stand on its own merits and should ask for no better thing than the full review of human life and need in the light of its interpretation. But it can only produce its fruits in a society where men are free to think and to act upon their sincere conviction. This means that Christianity calls for democracy, not as a specific political order but as essential freedom to think and to act upon the dictates of a conscience responsible ultimately and directly to God. Granted that no political machinery will ever give unhindered expression to such a principle, nevertheless the very existence of a free conscience before God demands the recognition of such freedom of conscience in personal life and in civic and political effort.

The world today is looking for national objectives. The specific form of national life must be worked out by trial and error and according to the culture and the external circumstances in any country. But the spiritual faith must be derived from man's insight and by virtue of his religious nature. Christianity claims to have the answer to this quest! But if the answer is to come in clear accents and if it is to be received by the world, certain things are required both of Christianity itself and of the world. Christianity must establish in theology the *truth* of its doctrine of God, upon which all else depends. And it must work constantly for the removal of obstacles to intellectual liberty and barriers to the essential democracy which free religion requires in order to bring men to a knowledge of God and to do its work of regeneration and peace in human society.

CHAPTER II

The Different Kinds of Religion

TO SUPPLY ANY HUMAN SOCIETY WITH IDEAL OBJECTIVES AND WITH a unifying faith that will give significance and value to human life, is the essential function of religion. But it must be a religion firmly believed to be true, and also competent to deal creatively with the deepest springs of human desire. The present demand is for a religion which can also guide human life in ways that make for world unity and righteousness. Such a requirement brings under critical review the present-day secular substitutes for religion, but it also brings up for a new and radical appraisal the religious systems themselves. Finally, when we make the assertion that Christianity has the answer to the world's demand for a living faith, we must honestly criticize all forms of Christianity to find which form actually existing or coming to be is that faith. Some hint of this type of criticism has been given already as regards the secular faiths and historic forms of Christianity. We turn now to the religions of the world to inquire into their competence for the role of unifying world faith.

Despite the fact that men are predominantly concerned today with great issues of social and economic reconstruction, it remains true that the most important issues are religious. Man's most profound attempts to solve the problem of life and destiny are to be found in the great religious systems. The whole man facing his total relation to the universe, to life and death, sin and righteousness, eternity and time, finds his security and hope in a religious faith. Beset by mystery within himself and all about him, he charts his course by gleams of divine light which reveal meaning and direction and ultimate destiny for his soul. Such insights come originally from seers and prophets and mystics, but there is in every man a capacity to share them and appropriate them for himself.

Philosophy, when it pushes beyond the limited area of its own techniques and faces the ultimate meaning of existence or the nature of reality, verges on the religious; it does in many cases develop into a cautious, skeptical, self-conscious kind of religion. And science, which is prohibited by its own rules from taking the comprehensive view, occasionally leads to mysteries that suggest religious ideas. Both science and philosophy contribute to the purifying and advancement of religion. Philosophy, especially, furnishes conceptual forms and rational criticism for religious thought; and science, especially in the fields of history and psychology, has rendered great service to religion. But religion is prior to both science and philosophy; it exists and will exist by grace of neither. It springs out of profound human need and a consciousness of being, more real and comprehensive than any ever to be attained in the critical, defining, analytical processes of philosophy, or by the factual, utilitarian operation of scientific thought. It is prior to both in point of time and in importance, for it embodies man's fundamental sense of worth and direction and the energy of spirit by which he lives. Errors in religion are more serious than errors in science or philosophy, for they are errors of heart and will as well as of idea. And truth in religion is most important of all, for it is truth in the realm of man's own spiritual nature and of his total adjustment to reality. What men really believe about God, or the nature of the God in whom men really believe and trust, is more potent in determining what men are than all their rational philosophy and objective science.

Religion and the religions, therefore, need to be studied with a new seriousness. In recent times a vast amount of learning has been devoted to historical and comparative studies in the field of religion. The academic task has been well done. Our interest now is not academic but intensely practical. We want an answer to this question: What religion or what form of religion can furnish the world with a unifying faith able to live in the light of free history and free science and lead men confidently to a conquest of the hates and fears that fill the world with foreboding? It is not necessary for us to be technical specialists or authorities in all the religions of the world to pursue this quest. The main characteristics of the major religions can be discovered and the fundamental differences between them brought to light. It is precisely these characteristics and distinctions that are important for our purposes.

Classified according to our present interest there are the following significant types of religion: (1) primitive, (2) ethnic, (3) national, and (4) universal.

Primitive religion is found among all races before the dawn of civilization. It is very much alike in all parts of the world. The African, the American Indian, the South Sea Islander, all have religious beliefs, practices, and functionaries, which are essentially alike. And in the early literature of advanced religions are to be found many survivals of this period. Indeed, one of the ever present problems in religion is the tendency of backward groups to return to the ways of man's naive nature religion. Perhaps it ought also to be said that primitive faith was not all error. It is, after all, the crude beginning of the most daring adventure of the human spirit. As science has grown out of magic, so spiritual religion has grown out of animism. There was something in man's original reaction to his mysterious environment which revealed a capacity for the religious development that followed. Today it has been estimated[1] that more than 160,000,000 people are still at this stage in culture and religion. As civilization and intellectual culture advance, this type of religion disappears, at least outwardly. Its superstitions are dispelled, not so much by the teaching of more advanced religions as by scientific knowledge. And the potency of science to dispel primitive beliefs lies not so much in its intellectual truth as in the fact that it works, that it enables men to do things that cannot be done by primitive magic.

But higher religious ideas are needed really to deliver men from primitive religion. It is not alone the external efficacy of natural science that is needed but a purification and exaltation of the idea of God. Primitive man suffers immeasurably from fear of unseen spiritual forces. Religion has never been merely utilitarian; there has also been in it a sense of personal relation with gods and spirits. An enlightened substitute for magic, which is the role of science, still leaves unresolved the more momentous issues of the environment of the soul. It may even intensify the terrors of men whose once unified conception of life now limps upon a half-enlightened knowledge. Security and confidence require belief in a God no less orderly and trustworthy than the nature which science reveals; that means a God morally just, but also fundamentally well disposed toward man, and that means a God of love.

It is characteristic of the prevailing secularism among church people today that many are more impressed by the fact that

[1] John Clark Archer, *Faiths Men Live By*, p. 2.

the Christian missionary gives the primitive peoples scientific enlightenment than by his primary religious service of teaching such peoples to know God as Christ reveals Him. The real spiritual poverty of these undeveloped peoples is not in their lack of scientific knowledge and control of natural forces, but in the thwarting of their own spirits through a dimmed and distorted vision of divinity.

The ethnic faith is a religion which is founded on race. The best known of such religions are Judaism and Hinduism. Even the names given to these religions reveal their racial character. Judaism is the religion of the Jews; Hinduism is the religion of the Hindus. The normal way to become a follower of an ethnic faith is to be born into the racial group whose religion it is. Provision is made in some ethnic religions for receiving proselytes. Such is the case, for example, with Judaism. But normally the people who hold such a faith look upon it as essentially a part of their racial inheritance. They do not expect or desire that men generally shall become adherents to it.

The attitude which I once heard expressed by a Jewish rabbi speaking to a Congregational conference is revealing. He argued that a man should remain in the religion into which he is born. If he is a Protestant he should be a good Protestant; if a Catholic, a good Catholic; and if a Jew, he should remain a good Jew. That is good and consistent doctrine for a representative of an ethnic faith. Let us make no mistake, however, as to the status it gives to religion; it quite definitely makes religion a part of one's racial or even family inheritance. It should not be necessary to point out that if such a principle had been followed consistently there never would have been a Protestant church. That would doubtless be considered a good thing by our Catholic friends. It is also true that if this principle had always prevailed there would never have been any Christianity. The first great crisis in the early days of Christianity arose over the question whether non-Jews could become disciples of Christ and members of the Church. Christianity broke away from Judaism on this issue—precisely because it would not live within the limits of an ethnic faith. It is perfectly consistent with his religious principle for a Jewish rabbi today to counsel any man to remain in the faith in which he was born, *because he was born in it;* it is equally consistent for the Christian, and indeed imperative, that he wholly reject such a conception. When Christian people question the validity of missions because, as they say, people should all remain undisturbed in the religion they already have, they ought to face squarely the fact that they are basing their argument upon the premises of an ethnic faith. They are arguing, perhaps, from the premises of Judaism but not from those of Christianity.

The strength of ethnic religion lies in its biological basis. Racial ties are ties of blood, and religion normally sanctifies and blesses those bonds. There is much of this even in Christianity and in a country where no established church or civil law creates a barrier to change from one form of the faith to another. Generally speaking, the Irishman is a Catholic, the Scotchman a Presbyterian, and the German a Lutheran. The Englishman is likely to be an Episcopalian, although that guess is less certain. All these guesses may be wrong, for many social, cultural and political cross-currents have interfered with the simplicity of the relation of religion to racial stock. But, even with all those influences at work, biology—or family—

still very largely determines at least nominal religious allegiance.

But if the biological basis strengthens the religious bond it also limits it and makes religion subservient to the prejudices and interests of racial groups. Perhaps the major handicap of Christianity in the Near East today is its identification with racial groups. Moslem Turkey knows Christianity too much in terms of its identification with such groups; Gregorian Christianity is Armenian; Orthodox Christianity is Greek, and Roman Catholic Christianity is French or Italian. This political character constitutes the most serious obstacle today to Protestant missionaries who at last are presenting Christianity in its own right without racial limitations and the consequent political implications.

There is another type of religion similar to but not identical with the ethnic, and that is *national* religion. At one time Judaism was a national as well as an ethnic religion, that is, so long as the Jewish State existed as a political unit. The ultimate goal or logic of Zionism points again in that direction. Certain forms of Christianity have been and in some cases still are national religions, for that is what a state church is. Lutheran Christianity is today the national religion of Sweden and Norway, and was formerly so in Germany; Anglican Christianity is the national religion of England; Roman Catholic Christianity was the religion of Austria. But there is a serious ambiguity in making any form of Christianity a national religion. To begin with, Christianity never can and never has, in principle, submitted to national limitation. Even when the ecclesiastical system is ultimately subject to control by the political state, as is still the case in England, the fact remains that both Church and State—in Christianity—derive their authority from God; and the knowledge of that God and His will comes historically by way of a tradition that has run through many channels and is essentially supernational.

There is another qualification of the national character even of a state church in the fact that other churches in other nations are also Christian. Indeed, the character of catholicity, or as we say now, ecumenicity, is so fundamental in Christianity that no sectarian or national claims can entirely conceal it. Apart from that is the fact that emigrants have carried with them to new lands their special form of faith and created churches which remain in communion with the state church in the fatherland. Lutheran Christianity may be the national religion of Sweden in Sweden, but the faith of a Swedish Lutheran congregation in Minnesota is not the national religion either of Sweden or of the United States. No form of Christianity can ever be a true national religion. If it could and would, in Germany today, the course of the Nazi regime would be simpler and the sufferings of German Christians much less.

The most perfect example of a national religion today is Shinto, which a Japanese scholar calls "the religion of the Japanese nation." Japanese nationalists today are the beneficiaries of an historical coincidence. They have at hand in the still surviving primitive faith of Shinto the perfect set-up for a religion of nationalism. European nations which have had centuries of intellectual enlightenment and which long ago abandoned their primitive mythologies for the cultural tradition stemming from Greece and the universal faith of Christianity, find it hard to create out-of-hand a plausible national religion. They are forced to do silly things and to make absurd claims. They must invent a new mythology and ritual to give emotional and intellectual support to their new faith. And although they do this with great enthusiasm it all has a hollow sound. It lacks the force of rational conviction and the dignity of an ancient custom.

But Japan suffers from no such disabilities. She does not have to invent a mythology, for she already has one in the ancient tradition of Shinto. Japan has emerged into the main stream of the world's life just at the time when political nationalism is attaining its highest intensity and becoming in effect a religion. And Japan, though she has assimilated the science and learning of the West, has not given up her heritage of faith. Shinto is still the state religion. It has its mythology and its shrines and its ritual. But more important still it has its deity, its God—the living Emperor of Japan. Here is nationalism supported by a religious faith deeply rooted in tradition and in the emotional life of the people. Small wonder that a shrewd government leadership has systematically revived and strengthened Shinto in recent years and made its system of universal primary education the means of teaching the essential Shinto doctrine of the divinity of the Emperor. For the divinity of the Emperor is the cornerstone of this whole structure. Nationalism anywhere means the deification of the political state. In most countries this is not easy to achieve. The state is a rather vague and elusive thing, it cannot be identified with the actual government, but must be posited as some mysterious entity existing behind and above the visible government. And it is impersonal. Neither Hitler nor Mussolini has yet dared to claim divinity. In this Germany and Italy are definitely at a disadvantage compared with Japan, whose first Emperor, according to Shinto mythology, was a descendant in the fifth generation of the sun goddess, Amaterasu-Omikami. Since the Japanese claim an unbroken imperial line from the very beginning, the present Emperor—Hirohito—is a god. Nor is that term used figuratively or by accommodation. Literally Hirohito is God and the highest God for the loyal Japanese subject. As described by the ardent Japanese nationalist, the relation of the people to their Emperor is filial and mystical even more than it is political. Or, in truth, the single relation of profound and passionate loyalty includes and transcends the political—it is religious.

Thus in Japan nationalism or the deification of the state is concrete and personal. Back of the actual political state is an exalted and divine person who *is* Japan. The State as a functioning political unit is his gracious gift to the Japanese people. At least that is the doctrine of Shinto. It represents the emotional if not always the intellectual attitude of the people generally. I asked a young Japanese if the educated men of Japan really believe in the divine descent of the Emperor. He shrugged his shoulders and said: "They may not believe in it as historic fact, but it is a very useful idea." No one dares to question it publicly. Indeed, there is a law which makes it a crime to say anything disrespectful of any member of the imperial family. Not even with all the weight of the tradition does the Japanese state feel it safe to permit free discussion of this cardinal point of the national religious faith. In this the religion of nationalism runs true to form.

But there is an inner contradiction in the idea of a national religion which is already apparent to many Japanese. It appears the moment Japan moves out of her own island realm populated by the Japanese and begins to exercise control over other peoples. For the Shinto conception of political government involves a relation between ruler and subject that is paternal, mystical, and religious. The Emperor is divine; in a lesser sense, but truly nevertheless, the people also are of a divine heaven-descended race. But Koreans are not of this race, nor are Formosans, yet both are now within the empire and therefore subject to the gracious rule of the Emperor. The self-sufficiency and the spiritual completeness of the Japanese nation thus breaks down. The very doctrine of a divine race and ruler which make the conquest of an empire seem such a holy cause, also makes true unity of the empire impossible. Perhaps that is one reason why Japan did not annex Manchukuo as she did Korea, but preferred to create a puppet state. She cannot recognize the Koreans or Formosans as equals of the Japanese in fact or in theory. Yet she must require of them loyalty to the Japanese Emperor. Here is a radical bar to the achievement of real unity in the empire and it is a bar created by the basic doctrine of the national faith.

This inner contradiction exists wherever nationalism becomes a religious faith. To be consistent, a country like Germany should gather all of the true German race within her national boundaries—if such a thing were possible—and then insulate them from the rest of the world. But the most conspicuous trait of current nationalism is its dominant tendency toward imperialism in spite of the fact that it has no inclusive conception of man and of political relations to undergird an empire. What an empire really does is to prove the insufficiency of the divine nation and to make its people dependent upon the profane parts and peoples of the earth.

Japan is destroying by her empire-building the doctrinal basis of her national religion and therefore of the Japanese state. Here is religion bound up with the fortunes of a national state, whatever they may be. The continuance of the nation proves the truth of the Shinto dogma and the dogma gives assurance of the permanence of the nation. If the nation should cease as an independent political state the religion of Shinto would be destroyed. This is clearly and positively stated by Professor Genchi Kato in his book (published in 1926) entitled *A Study of Shinto, The Religion of the Japanese Nation.*

The people have since (the defeat of the Mongols) entertained a feeling of national pride and strong faith that Japan, of all nations under the sun, is unique, rejoicing in the divine rule of one and the same Imperial dynasty, unbroken and co-eternal with Heaven and Earth.

Needless to add, such being the case, the people of Japan cannot help believing in the Providence of unseen help of the national deities on high; and that, *ipso facto,* Shinto, as the national religion still living, will be alive forever, as long as the nation of Japan flourishes and ceases not to exist.

Yahwism, the national religion of Israel, gave way to the universal religion of Christianity, along with the cessation of the existence of the nation of Israel; while Shinto, as the national religion of Japan, has continued and will continue, because Japan as a nation has continued and will continue. Here we see the difference between the national religion of the Jews and that of the Japanese people, although each may be called a "chosen people," and just therein exists one of the essential characteristics of Shinto.[2]

It is not difficult to see that such a conception is entirely inconsistent with Christianity. And this has been and is increasingly a problem for both the Christian Church in Japan

[2] P. 200.

and the Japanese Government. A technical solution has been reached but it by no means disposes of the fundamental conflict of doctrine. The constitution of modern Japan given by the Emperor Meiji in 1889 guarantees religious freedom. That guarantee was soon seen to be inconsistent with the religious character of Japanese patriotism which really requires that every loyal Japanese shall be a Shintoist. To meet this dilemma the government has ruled that state Shinto is not a religion. This Professor Kato calls the "secularizing of Shinto." This was made possible by distinguishing between two kinds of Shinto, state or shrine Shinto, and sect Shinto. The former is the national cult which uses the shrines and centers in a ritual of reverence to the living Emperor and his dead ancestors. The latter is the faith of voluntary groups or sects, of which thirteen are officially recognized. These sects are somewhat comparable to Protestant denominations in America. They are not permitted to use the Shinto shrines, but provide their own meeting halls. These sects are distinctly religious. They have services of preaching and worship and propagandize for their distinctive doctrines. They are closely watched by the state. Because they show a tendency for the religious spirit to go beyond the bounds of state doctrine occasionally one of the sects is suppressed. But this kind of Shinto, as contrasted with the state cult, is recognized as religious and no one is under any compulsion to accept its teachings or adhere to it in any of its forms.

Christians have taken full advantage of the distinction and have conformed to the requirements of the state cult with the understanding that their bowing before the shrine is an act of patriotic loyalty rather than religious worship. But, in fact, the conflict goes deeper; it has to do with the supreme commitment of life and with ultimate moral and spiritual allegiance. It is not really a matter of official terms, but of spiritual loyalties. The net effect of the secularizing of Shinto is to make it supreme and give it a solid advantage over all religions that are merely religions. This strategy is explained by Professor Kato as follows: "After the Restoration of 1868, the Meiji Government finally proclaimed State Shinto as non-religious; and in 1884, put it entirely apart from the Buddhistic and Christian religions and gave it a sphere of independent existence quite different from that of the foreign religions, thus furnishing State Shinto with an asylum in which, under the protective aegis of the political power of the secular Government, it is safe from interference by its two religious rivals."[3] This could be done, according to Professor Kato, "because in Shinto, or, more strictly speaking, in State Shinto, where the theanthropic expression of religion predominates as it does in the religions of ancient Greece and Rome, the object of worship is a secular ruler on earth in flesh and blood."

Thus we have still in the world primitive, ethnic, and national religions. There are also universal religions of which the important ones are Buddhism, Mohammedanism, and Christianity. Primitive religion is a natural, almost instinctive response of the human spirit to life, interpreting nature in terms of its own interests and feelings and filling in the blank spaces, especially the dread darkness caused by death, with the pictures created by imagination. No critical line is drawn between fact and imagination. The vital impulse produces and is satisfied with a concrete spiritual order conceived in terms essentially akin to those of earthly existence. This primitive

[3] Genchi Kato, *A Study of Shinto, The Religion of the Japanese Nation,* p. 210.

faith may, in some respects, be profoundly true; but it is in detail illusory, and it is open to extremes of superstition and both spiritual and moral perversion.

Primitive religion recedes with the growth of civilization and culture. Its simplicity and homogeneity are broken up. Racial genius, the positive influence upon belief and conduct of strong individuals, and the whole complex of conditions in a developing society (including climate and geography, the economic basis of life, commerce and cultural exchange with other peoples)—all these factors enter in to create a racial culture of which religion is an integral part. Thus comes into being the ethnic faith.

When a racial group is isolated geographically and becomes also a single political unit, as in the case of Japan, or when a tribe or group of tribes develops into a separate nation as did the people of Israel, the ethnic faith becomes also a national religion. But the two are not identical. The basis of ethnic religion is biological; that of a national religion is political. As we have already seen it is impossible to keep these two boundaries identical.

Thus the basis of primitive religion is instinct, that of ethnic faith is biology, and that of national religion is politics. What, then, is the basis of universal religion? Wherein are the universal religions different from the other three types?

The most obvious difference, of course, is that the universal religion is not either actually or in principle limited to any racial stock or political unit; its nature is to pass all such limits and to include all who will accept it. There is a sort of unconscious universality in primitive religion, essentially similar beliefs and practices appearing in various parts of the world in the first stages of human culture, since human nature is fundamentally the same. But this is by no conscious intent or purpose; it is simply a naive, uncritical assertion of the human spirit. The universal religions, however, represent the mature fruit of a long course of moral and intellectual development. Their bid for acceptance by all men, everywhere, is based upon the claim that they have the truth about the spiritual nature of man and the universe in which he lives. Truth, like human nature, must be the same for all men. Race and nationality are relatively superficial. Man is of one blood and one spirit. Geography and climate vary; nature is essentially the same. Customs and standards are diverse; virtue at heart is constant. And so God or the ultimate spiritual Reality, to whom the human spirit owes supreme allegiance and in whom it finds its true home, is one. The universal religion is *universal* because it claims to be *true*. It is not a set of mores, nor a part of the complex of a racial culture, much less the divine sanction of a national state. It is a teaching about God and man, a way of salvation for man, a faith whose validity rests upon its essential veracity in dealing with the momentous issue of the nature of man's essential being and his relation to God. Religion as truth is as universal as physics or astronomy or scientific medicine. And Islam, Buddhism, and Christianity are universal religions because they claim to be true.

Universal religions, therefore, are inevitably rivals. No matter how much the Buddhist, the Moslem, and the Christian love each other—and by the tenets of at least two of these they should love each other—no matter how much they appreciate and even admire certain particular things in the other faiths, the fact remains that each must challenge the others at certain points as either untrue or only partially and inadequately true.

At this point the average man will throw up his hands in despair. How is it possible for anyone ever to deal intelligently with such a subtle and complex problem? And, remembering the fruitless battle of dogmas in past centuries, the modern man is likely to shun the whole issue as hopeless and irrelevant. But it is neither hopeless nor irrelevant, and it is not beyond the capacity of the ordinarily intelligent man to arrive at an understanding of religion and to judge between the doctrines offered him by these rivals for the world's faith.

As a matter of fact the centuries of argument which seem to us so futile did clear the way for a new and more direct approach to religious faith. Dogma and myth have been pitted against dogma and myth with no other claim to support on either side than revelation and tradition. Now we do not deny the essential fact of revelation today, nor the value of tradition, but we claim freedom of mind and spirit to examine all revelations and traditions and to use both intelligence and spiritual insight as a basis for acceptance or rejection. Moreover, we live in the same universe as did those who created the tradition, we have the same nature, and are in the presence of the same God from whom came the original revelations. The pure in heart can still see God; the honest mind can still arrive at the truth about Him. There are no closed canons of revelation. Man is face to face with God; the facts of nature including human nature are open to our view. We can and must today seek the truth in religion, and we must decide between conflicting claims made by the religions which, being universal, base their appeal upon the claim to truth.

In the discussion of religion and the world mission of Christianity which follows, I shall attempt to indicate at least some of the criteria of religious truth and validity, not in abstract terms, but in terms of the concrete character and fruits in life of the religions of the world. To grasp and understand truth in religion, one must see it not alone in rational statement, but in ethical and social embodiment. It is, after all, a truth about life and has as much to do with feelings and will, with the social bond and the ultimate satisfactions of life, as it does with a rational order of ideas; indeed more, for life is the substance, and concepts but the reflected form of reality.

Especially does the demand of the peoples of the world today for a working faith make this quest for a true religion, not private or academic, but an urgent practical enterprise. What is the true faith for the world? Certainly we cannot rest in an ethnic or national religion. They support and sanction the very divisions of men which create endless conflict. They cannot be wholly true. Mankind can find its unifying faith only in a universal religion. And that religion must be honestly and intelligently believed in; it must give an essentially true account of the nature of man; it must reveal the true basis of community. It must have both metaphysical and social validity. And these go together, for it is inconceivable that the truth about human nature should be independent of, to say nothing of being inconsistent with, the truth about the nature of the universe. One of the most vital points in the operation of any religion is the consequence of its main metaphysical doctrines in human conduct and in social organization. In the next chapter I shall try to show what those consequences are in some of the world's great religious systems.

CHAPTER III

The Role of Religion in Human Life

EVERY GREAT RELIGION EXPRESSES SOME PRINCIPLE, SOME CENTRAL and regulative idea which pervades all particular beliefs and forms of expression and gives the main direction to its influence upon the life of its followers. The spiritual climate is determined by this inner principle, the way people feel, and the attitudes they take toward life, the way they think about themselves, the spirit in which they face the duties and varied fortunes of existence. This regulative idea or principle is of such pervasive importance that we fail to understand any religion until we have discovered and defined it. Much of the comparative study of religions is absorbed with specific beliefs, rituals, and forms of organized worship, and with the details of practical conduct which are prescribed by or result from religious teaching. This is all valuable and indispensable. A religion is a concrete, historic fact and it must be known in its specific features. But often the general character of a religion in its determinative influence upon human life is lost in this study. To get a comparative picture of real significance we must find and set side by side the principles by which the different faiths affect the conduct of men. By doing this we shall have a vantage point from which we may discuss both the truth of any religion and its practical value for human life.

HINDUISM

Hinduism is one of the most baffling religious systems in the world. One might despair of ever finding any single idea or principle in it. Every kind of religion seems to be discover-able in the total complex of what is loosely called Hinduism. To begin with, while it is legitimately called an ethnic faith, its philosophers and theologians have from ancient times moved in a realm of abstract speculation which takes no account of racial peculiarities. Not only does this free speculation on the ultimate nature of Reality ignore all limits of race or racial culture; it includes diverse and incongruous doctrines. If one asks: Is Hinduism monotheistic or polytheistic?, the answer is, both. Jawaharlal Nehru, in his *Autobiography*, says: "One may even be a professing atheist—as the old Hindu philosopher, Charvarka, was—and yet no one dare to say that he has ceased to be a Hindu. Hinduism clings on to its children, almost despite them." One may be a pantheist, a theist, or even an atheist and still be a Hindu. One may worship in a temple or never enter a temple, and yet be a Hindu. One may worship in any one or in several of a bewildering multiplicity of forms, or not worship at all, and be a good Hindu. One may be an ascetic or indulge in all the delights of the flesh that he can afford; he is in both cases a Hindu.

Apparently the regulative principle of Hinduism is not found in theology, in forms of worship, or in moral standards. Contradictions in these things do not violate that principle. The reason is that the constitutive factor in Hinduism is the social system itself. So long as one conforms to that he is a Hindu in good standing whatever his belief or lack of belief, his fault or virtue, as judged by general moral standards. One may cease to believe in God but one may not marry out of one's caste. The breakdown of the caste system would be the essential disintegration of Hinduism. Hinduism *is* funda-mentally a social system. That is why Gandhi, while he would remove its abuses, upholds the caste system itself as good.

Gandhi is essentially an Indian nationalist; accordingly he wants all Hindus to be true to Hinduism. But that means, true to the social order which is Hinduism. If all Hindus should accept Gandhi's high conception of life and his interpretation of caste it would mean a spiritual revolution in India. But it would not mean the abandoning of caste.

Here is one pronounced form of the social expression of religion. It is an extreme form, since in Hinduism social structure *is* the basic element of religion, the one ultimate mark of membership. Religion makes its impact upon life both individual and social by imposing and maintaining caste. It furnishes the pervasive and dominant framework within which the Hindu, whatever his personal belief or disbelief, must live. This is its source of strength. It is endlessly tolerant of vagaries in theology, but unyielding in its demand for social conformity, because if it yields there Hinduism ceases to be.

ISLAM

Perhaps the most significant terms to designate the Mohammedan faith is that used by Charles R. Watson in his book, *What Is This Moslem World?* He says that "Islam can be truly described as totalitarian."[1] Recent political developments have made us familiar with the totalitarian state. It is a state which assumes direct control over all aspects of life, which governs not by general laws within which individuals and groups may live their lives in their own way. The totalitarian state regulates specifically business and industry, and also education, art, sports, and even science and religion. The political

[1] Charles R. Watson, *What Is This Moslem World?* (Friendship Press) p. 53.

power reaches into every area of human thought, feeling, and action, and prescribes the norm and standard.

This is a new and rather appalling thing in political government; but it is really as old as Islam. In Islam there is no mere framework of general principles; there is specific law for every important relation of human life. There is no distinction between religious and secular; all life is religious. Viewed in one way that is a good thing. However, before hastily assuming that in this Islam has expressed the true character and function of religion, let us see just what it means. It means, for one thing, that Islam is a political state, a theocracy. It is a state whose ruler is Allah. The first earthly representative of Allah was Mohammed who received the directions of the divine will by revelation. Since Mohammed the Moslem state has been ruled by the caliphs, or successors to Mohammed. It means, also, that Islam is a theology. This is natural to religion; but Islam is also a philosophy. Like the mediaeval Catholic Church, Moslem thinkers took Aristotle as their teacher in philosophy, but used his rules to rationalize and establish the truth of religion. Islam, further, is a legal system. The civil and criminal codes are a part of the Moslem system of life. This also prescribes the social system, the nature of family life, and all man's relations to his fellows. Moslem morality, therefore, is detailed and concrete. But Islam reaches beyond law and morals and into the domain of culture. Literature and art are as definitely Moslem as is theology. The Koran, written in the Arabic language, furnishes both a language of culture and literary norms. The Arabic of the Koran is God's Arabic! The prohibition of all representation of living beings as tending to idolatry created a distinctive Moslem art in which geometrical designs and the Arabic script are the chief motifs. That is where we get the term "arabesque" as we get many other words and forms from Moslem culture.

Islam is not, therefore, just a "religion" in any limited meaning of the word. It is also a philosophy, a political state (at least in tradition and theory), a legal code, a morality, a social system, and a literary and artistic culture. Its relation to human life is one of comprehensive and specific control. This has given great strength and social solidarity to the Moslem fellowship. It is one of the main reasons why Christianity has made such slow progress in winning converts from Islam. There are no points at which the Moslem soul ranges free to find and test a new way.

But the difficulties of such a system are very great. It tends powerfully to a rigid conservatism such as actually has overtaken Islam. If a revealed law is definite that means that its specific form does not change. But life does change. A system of moral and social regulations sufficient for a simple Arab society of the seventh century was soon strained by the expansion of Islam over much of Asia, Africa, and Europe, and by the rapid development of wealth and culture. To provide for all this change and growing complexity Islam had to resort to an elaborate system of casuistry. The lawyer became and still remains of great importance in Moslem life. A similar development occurred in mediaeval Europe when Catholic canon law tried to meet all the practical issues of life by deducing specific rules from the revealed truths and precepts of religion. Such a system not only becomes top-heavy but offers many avenues of escape from duty which subtle minds and minds not so subtle can easily discover. It tends to corrupt the quality of moral life.

Another difficulty is encountered when the Moslem state

loses its independence and sovereignty. As we have seen, the Moslem system requires a political state ruled by a caliph whose function is primarily that of interpreter and administrator of the will of Allah. The chief schism in Islam—that between sunnites and shiites—was caused by a difference over the question of succession to the caliphate. Any full-fledged Moslem society must have a caliph and a political government under his rule. This all sounds unreal today since most Moslems are subject to nominally Christian states. That situation was bad enough when there was in Turkey a real political ruler, the sultan, who was also the caliph and so in theory the head of all Islam. But even that shadow of a caliphate vanished during and after the world war. Moslems in India and Arabia not only refused to follow the sultan-caliph and fight for the Ottoman Empire, but they enlisted under the banner of the Allies and helped to bring about his defeat. Then the modern Turkish state emerged. It first separated the caliphate from the sultanate, and then banished the caliph from Istanbul. Since then the Moslem world has been politically headless and the last vestige of Islam as a government has disappeared.

That seems to be what history does to theocracies. The only one still remaining is in Japan, and what will happen to it no one can tell, although this seems to be a time of crisis there. However, our purpose here is not to speculate on the possible continuance of theocracy but to point out the totalitarian character of the Moslem religion, of which the theocratic state was one integral element. It is the most impressive example of a religion whose relation to human life is one of legal prescription in regard to belief and worship and all forms of personal and social conduct. It has all the strength and all the spiritual futility of such a system.

A contemporary Moslem scholar says that "During the last five hundred years religious thought in Islam has been practically stationary"[2]; and Syed Ameer Ali wrote more than twenty years ago that the protestant reformation in Islam is only just commencing.[3] Whether the reawakening and reformation of Islam can accomplish the thing these liberals desire is an open question. If it does succeed and if, as Sir Mohammed Iqbal says is necessary, the younger generation should "examine, in an independent spirit, what Europe has thought and how far the conclusions reached by her can help us in the revision and, if necessary, reconstruction of theological thought in Islam,"[4] it would complete the disintegration of Islam as a totalitarian religion. And that would finally destroy the classic answer the Moslem faith has given to the practical question as to how religion should exercise a saving influence in human life.

BUDDHISM

Buddhism stands at the opposite pole from Islam and Hinduism. Both of the latter exercise on principle a positive control of human life, Hinduism through the caste system, which is of its essence, and Islam by its totalitarian authority. But in principle Buddhism has nothing to do with the organization and conduct of human life. This is a difficult doctrine for most of us to understand, but a brief statement of certain Buddhist ideas will make it clear that Buddhism could consistently come to no other issue about the earthly life of man.

Buddhism has been described as "a life- and world-denying

[2] Sir Mohammed Iqbal, *The Reconstruction of Religious Thought in Islam* (Oxford University Press), p. 6.
[3] *The Spirit of Islam*, p. 328.
[4] Sir Mohammed Iqbal, *op. cit.*, p. 7.

religion."[5] To make evident the meaning of this a contrast will help. In the first chapter of Genesis, after the account of creation comes this declaration: "And God saw everything that he had made and, behold, it was very good." This may be taken as a classic phrase of world- and life-affirmation. Whatever natural and moral evil may be found in the world, Judeo-Christianity by its doctrine of divine creation holds that the world and life are essentially good, that the gifts of God are to be received with gratitude, and life is to be lived so that God's good will shall be done among men. No personal or national sufferings have ever been able to destroy this faith. Jews and Christians have had their share of both kinds of suffering, and have wrestled with the problem of evil in all its aspects. The book of Job faces unflinchingly the hard fact of unmerited suffering and achieves a new height of faith in God: "Though He slay me yet will I trust Him." And Christianity finds the insight of Hosea and the ideal of the suffering servant of Jehovah historically realized in the crucified Christ. The vicarious suffering of the righteous is declared to be the price and power of redemptive love.

Thus Judeo-Christianity remains world- and life-affirming in the face of the full impact of suffering. But Buddhism finds no way to transmute or conquer evil, but only a way to escape it. It conceives of the earthly life as essentially evil, and seeks salvation by complete denial of it and escape from it. The four great truths of Buddhism are (1) all life is suffering, (2) suffering is born of desire, (3) salvation is the extinction of desire, (4) the way to deliverance is the noble eight-fold path of moral and psychological discipline. This is the classic statement of life- and world-negation. Christ said: "I came that

[5] Albert Schweitzer, *Indian Thought and Its Development*.

they may have life, and may have it abundantly." But Buddhism comes not that men may have life in abundance but that they may find release from life.

Or, to put it in another way, Buddhism is profoundly pessimistic about life; Christianity is correspondingly optimistic. Buddhism sees no issue to life but suffering; in the face of all suffering Christianity is hopeful. Buddhism despairs completely of life and teaches a technique by which the individual may ultimately be free from the burden of life. Popular Buddhism has departed far from the original doctrine in many respects, but not in this. Religion is still, even among the common people, a doctrine of defense against and deliverance from life.

This gives the real reason why Buddhism has no responsibility for the ordering of life in an earthly society. It has no principle of moral regeneration either for the individual or—much less—for society. This is apparent to those who live in intimate contact with Buddhism even at its best, for example in Japan, where Buddhism is today more enlightened and on a higher plane generally than in any other country. It is more progressive there and has responded more constructively to the challenge of modern thought and Christian ideals. Japanese Buddhism has adopted many of the practical forms and expressions of protestant Christianity. There are Young Men's Christian Associations and Sunday schools which not only follow the organization and programs of their Christian prototypes but also inculcate some of the Christian ideas. There are also many social centers usually attached to Buddhist temples and using the best modern techniques. This frank imitation of Christian forms of practical service is a credit to Japanese Buddhism and a thing to be welcomed. But it can very easily obscure the fundamental difference in principle between the two religions.

I raised the question in Japan with several groups of Christian pastors whether Buddhism did not give promise of furnishing the moral motivation and the spiritual power that Japan needs. Specifically I asked whether the Japanese Buddhist who becomes a Christian is a better man morally. I found no disposition to denounce Buddhism on the part of these Christian pastors. Some of them had been Buddhists and all spoke appreciatively of its spiritual truths and values. But they were quite positive in saying that the Christian convert from Buddhism is definitely a better man morally and that Buddhism had no answer to the moral and social needs of the nation. They all agreed that "Buddhism is lacking in moral imperative and dynamic." That phrase was repeated more than once, and I carried it in my mind as a mature judgment of informed Christian leaders upon Buddhism.

But I was not fully satisfied to take such a judgment as final, coming as it did from Christian preachers. It is natural and pardonable that the professional representatives of the Christian faith in a predominantly Buddhist environment should be biassed. It is not to be wondered at if they are inclined to underrate its chief rival. I was glad, therefore, to be able to submit their statement to a distinguished Buddhist scholar. In Kyoto I had the rare privilege of a long conversation with Professor D. T. Suzuki. I went to his home with Dr. Edward S. Cobb, of the Doshisha University. Dr. Suzuki is a follower of the Zen sect of Buddhism. He is well known in this country, which he has visited more than once, because of his writings in English on Zen Buddhism.

After an hour of friendly and unargumentative discussion

of Christianity and Buddhist philosophy, I ventured to put before Dr. Suzuki the thing the Christian pastors had told me and to ask for his frank opinion of it. He replied: "Yes, I should agree with them that Buddhism is lacking in moral imperative and dynamic, and not only among the common people, but among educated Buddhists also. But you must remember that in Buddhism, religion is not interested in morality, for morality is a matter of personal effort and social relations, and in Buddhism religion is not interested in those things but in the soul and its salvation." Dr. Cobb then remarked: "Then you mean that in Buddhism salvation is a change of state but not of character," and Dr. Suzuki answered: "Yes."

Now this statement can easily be misconstrued and it needs to be analyzed and related to the basic doctrine of Buddhism to be understood. It does not mean, of course, that Buddhism has never taught moral standards and discipline, but it does indicate a radically different relation between religion and morality from that which we find in Judaism and Christianity. Buddhism does teach a moral discipline as part of the noble eight-fold path. But more important is its teaching of pity or compassion for all living things. That doctrine has leavened oriental societies and has been a softening and refining influence wherever Buddhism has gone.

However, the Buddhist doctrine both gives a peculiar meaning to love and puts definite limits upon it. Since the Buddhist despairs of life, compassion for his fellows takes the form of pity for those in a hopeless state and a desire to help them find the way of escape from it. Love is not a motive and guide for conduct in human society to the end that the common life may be made blessed, but an impulse to help others find the way of deliverance from life. Love, therefore, is not the law of life or the principle of community. The limit put on love was brought out by James Bissett Pratt in his conversations with Buddhists during his travels in the Orient.

One of the monks had rehearsed to me, quite correctly, the Four Noble Truths, and I had brought him back by further questions to the fact that desire is the cause of sorrow and that it is the aim of Buddhism to avoid sorrow. Does this desire, I asked, include love for other people and desire for their welfare? Yes, he replied: love—love quite as much as hate—is one of the causes of sorrow. Then, said I, we ought not to love each other or desire each other's welfare? Oh, yes, he said, Buddhism teaches us to love each other and to desire the welfare of all. When I pointed out the fact that he had contradicted himself he recognized it, but that what he meant was this: We ought to get rid of love quite as much as hate, but we cannot fully do so till we reach Nibban. It is really wrong to love other people and we should seek to avoid both love and hate. One of the other monks, standing by, was quite dissatisfied by this admission and tried to save the situation by making a distinction. There are two kinds of love, he said, sex love and love for people's welfare, the desire to do them good and help them. Sex love is bad, love for people's welfare is good. But, I asked, does this second kind of love bring sorrow—when, for example, those one loves are ill or die, or when the good we desire for them cannot be attained. He admitted that this kind of love also may and often does bring sorrow; only, he said, this is unavoidable. I pointed out that its unavoidability, if true, is quite irrelevant. So he followed his predecessor in admitting that we really ought to get rid of both kinds of love.[6]

Here is a striking difference between the Christian and the Buddhist meaning of love. In Christianity love is the permanent motivation of life and it is the power that makes life

[6] *The Pilgrimage of Buddhism* (Macmillan Company), p. 175.

eternally worth living. It is the true bond between persons and is therefore essentially ethical and social in character. It abides, it is "the greatest of these," it "never faileth." But in Buddhism love does not abide; it must be sacrificed to enlightenment. It is not the greatest and it must fail before religion can effect its perfect work of salvation. The finest ethical principle of Buddhism must be abandoned so that religion can succeed. This tragic disjunction between religion and morality is the fatal weakness of Buddhism. It is not a failure of the faith to fulfil itself, but is due to the metaphysics of Buddhism. There is therefore little reason to hope that Buddhism will ever really overcome it.

When Professor Suzuki gave that rather surprising confirmation to the statement of Christian pastors, he was not confessing a failure of Buddhism but making a positive affirmation as to its intrinsic character. He accurately defined the nature and the realm of morality which is "a matter of personal effort and social relations." But personal effort is futile for the Buddhist and the individual must separate himself from social ties to find salvation. Effort and social relations are of the substance of life and life itself is an evil to be destroyed. Religion therefore, in Buddhism, cannot do anything for one except to teach him how to cease his own effort and disentangle himself from society so that he may find salvation.

Not the full doctrine but the essential separation between religion and morality is found in the popular Buddhism. Professor Tamomatsu of Keio University, preaching from a Tokyo radio station, put it in less technical but more striking form than did Mr. Suzuki. In substance this was his argument: "Christianity is hard to believe; it tries to convert; Buddhism is easy because it does not want to reconstruct lives.

You need a ticket to get into Christianity. Buddhism you get in free."

Naturally a religion that despairs of the world and that looks upon the very desire for life as the source of all evil cannot have in it a redeeming ideal and motivation for life. Buddhism has at best but a negative relation to human life. It provides only a belief and a cult by which the individual may be fortified so as to endure life as long as necessary and by which he may eventually escape from it entirely.

In this brief survey of the way in which religions are related to life we have gone from one extreme to another. In Hinduism and even more in Islam life in its essential aspects is absorbed into the structure of religion. In Buddhism religion renounces life and offers a salvation of escape from it. We now turn to Christianity to inquire into its principle of effective control in human society.

CHRISTIANITY

I have used the term "Judeo-Christianity," for the history of Christianity is continuous with that of Judaism and Christians have always claimed that their faith is the true and logical fulfilment of Jewish doctrine. In the matter now being discussed the essential principle is the same, for Judaism ceased to be a totalitarian religion with the Captivity and there were within it long before the coming of Christ the well-developed doctrines of a truly ethical faith. It is that element which Christianity inherited and to which it gave its own distinctive form. The principle of Christianity is that of an ethical religion or of a religious morality. This is of vital importance today, when the world is looking for a faith which is both rooted in religion and realistic in regard to the facts and needs of human life.

The regulative principle in Hinduism is the social system itself. Islam is totalitarian religion which absorbs and dominates the whole of life in principle and in specific detail. Buddhism renounces all social responsibility and leaves society to find its way in this present evil life. Christianity is an ethical religion which has a permanent motivation for life and furnishes essential conceptions and ideals for the regeneration of the individual and society. Its moral imperative and dynamic spring directly and inevitably from its essential character as a religion.

Before discussing this principle of Christianity it must be remarked that historically each of the attitudes which mark the characteristic relation of religion to life in the three non-Christian religions which we have been discussing is to be found at some time and in some degree in Christianity. While no Christian communion has ever officially stated that being a Christian consists primarily in social conformity, that has been and still actually is a very wide-spread practical attitude. At least so far as having status in the Church is concerned, the force of social orthodoxy is very great. One wonders whether a church member who married a Negro—in states where such marriage is legal—could remain in good standing in a Protestant congregation. He would be ostracised in most cases as having violated the most radical caste restriction. It would be little less tolerable in many churches for a member to join the Communist party. Nor in this case would it be the matter of doctrine—communists being atheists—but the social offense that would bar the communist from Christian fellowship.

Now, I am not commending either intermarriage between

whites and Negroes, nor the joining of the Communist party, but only pointing out that the offense against Christianity in both cases is essentially an offense against a social system rather than a matter of faith or morals. In the case of inter-marriage it is entirely such an offense. Even in the case of a defection to communism it is not the atheism that breaks the bond. Many church members have friends, often in academic circles but also in other cultured groups, who are atheists so far as religious belief is concerned. But such un-believers, while usually not formally members of the Church, are under no social ban. Like the Hindus we are much more tolerant of religious unbelief, and even of moral laxity, than of social non-conformity. It should be pointed out, however, that this is not a natural fruit of the Christian conception of life, but a result of the natural pride of man and his fear lest his security founded on a specific social order be threatened.

As has been suggested above, medieval Christianity was in effect a totalitarian religion. It would be so today if the Roman Catholic Church could have its way. Then the Pope was not himself the ruler of the Holy Roman Empire, but he had the right to consecrate and he claimed authority to depose the emperor. Aside from this always disputed relation of the spiritual to the secular power, the Church exercised a dominant control over the minds as well as the outward actions of its members, and exercised censorship over all forms of art as well. Both nationalism and secularism have had at least the negative virtue of a successful challenge to this totalitarian form of Christianity. The result of this has been to compel Catholic Christianity to accept a new relation to secular af-fairs. Ever since the rejection by European states in the Peace of Westphalia (1648) of the right of the Church to interfere in the making of treaties, it has been fighting a losing fight for a voice in international politics, and only in 1929, in the agreement between the Pope and Mussolini called the Lateran Accord, did the Roman Church finally and formally renounce such claim to direct intervention in international affairs.[7]

The freeing of men's minds in general has made for progress in science and philosophy and a certain realism in all the practical affairs of life. The free mind has done its work in these matters; it was a work of empirical exploration and experimentation. Now men everywhere are coming to the realization that they need a meaning for life that this method of discovery and experiment does not disclose. It provides means but not ends, and mankind must find worthy ends to live for. But this is the realm of religion. Christianity again is called upon to provide a positive ideal and objective for human life, but it must exercise its control in a manner intrinsic to its own nature, and that is not the way of totalitarianism.

The Buddhist principle also has had its expression in Christendom. There is a legitimate other-worldliness in Christianity and a realism regarding human nature that have often produced an attitude of despair of the world and a renunciation of any moral responsibility for it. Monasticism in the Catholic Church, and no less the purely individualistic idea of salvation that has prevailed so largely in Protestantism, both grow out of this attitude. All apocalypticism is born of a similar pessimism. But Christianity cannot be resolved into a religion of escape from the world or complete pessimism as to its future, because Christianity is fundamentally ethical and

[7] See *The Papacy and World Affairs*, by Carl Conrad Eckhardt (University of Chicago Press), for a full treatment of this subject.

its ethics is not merely personal but social as well. It must preserve the tension and paradox of a faith rooted in the divine and pledged to the complete redemption of the human race. Being ethical, the Christian religion does have to do with human effort and social relations which Professor Suzuki correctly designates as the sphere of morality.

Hinduism identifies religion with the social system and so sanctions the *status quo*. Islam, by exercising a pervasive authority, creates an arbitrary and essentially conservative control. Buddhism abandons human life to other influences. The true relation of religion to life in Christianity is none of these. Its character as ethical prescribes the main terms of that relation. Now the essence of moral conduct is freedom. Only a person acting by his own free will is truly moral. Arbitrary control by a social system or legal authority destroys this moral quality. Christianity by its own principle must take the risks of freedom. It must win the heart and will before it can rule. But in so far as it succeeds it has created a person and a society in which righteousness is real, and produced by a motive that can cope with obstacles and changes, and ceaselessly devise new and better ways to attain its objective. Christianity is leaven in human society; it works by a renewal of the inner life and by the persistent appeal of its ideal of human brotherhood.

Christianity does not operate by direct compulsion on human conduct. When a church or a "Christian" government imposes and enforces a "Christian morality" that is not Christianity. It is a legal reflection of Christianity but not Christianity itself, for Christianity is not a principle of specific control applying either to all aspects of society or to all the members of society. It works through the minority who not only con-

form to Christian personal and social standards of morality
but who also have in their hearts free enthusiasm for its ideal

More is required of Christian men and of the Christian
Church than of any other system, if Christianity is to furnish
the world with a saving faith. Christians must *be* the salt
of the earth; the Church must *be* a city set on a hill; Christianity lived must *be* the lamp set on a table to lighten all
that are in the house. There is no doubt that Christianity is
the one faith that can unify and redeem life, but it does not
work officially or automatically; it works through the lives
and through the fellowship of those who believe in it with all
their hearts and who are true to it whatever the strength of
the opposition.

CHAPTER IV

The Effect of Religion on Civilization

WE HAVE ALREADY NOTED IN THE PREVALENCE OF ONE-PARTY governments a striking evidence of the need of national groups for a faith as well as a form of life—a faith which will give value both to the individual and to the nation. Since such a faith is in effect a religion, this means that the world is again, from a new angle of approach, asserting its need of religion. In the light of that asserted need we have surveyed the different types of religion and then examined three major non-Christian faiths and Christianity itself to discover the principle by which each one relates itself to the life of man. In the light of this preliminary study we now turn to the actual effects of different religions on the civilizations where they have had time and opportunity to produce characteristic results.

Since the Christian religion itself was once the real spiritual bond of unity in western Europe, we have to face squarely and candidly the reason, so far as it may be found within organized Christianity, for the progressive deterioration it has exhibited in that role during the past few centuries. For whatever it once may have been there is no doubt that Christianity eventually assumed a form which made it incapable of coping with, to say nothing of guiding and leading the new life that stirred the peoples of Europe. Christianity had become a Church with worldly wealth and political power and ambition. Its authority in human affairs was too largely exerted, not for the advancement of Christian social and ethical ideals, but for the defence of its own secular interests. Christianity also had become a dogma that resisted and anathematized that free intellectual activity which has created the modern world. The story does not need to be retold of the dogmatic conservatism which made it necessary for Europe to defy the Church in order to develop both politically and intellectually. We are seeing the danger today of a self-sufficient nationalism and the inadequacy of a secular intellectualism. However, we must not overlook or minimize the social progress made during the past few centuries, and the vast and real benefits that have come from a mental activity, not alone in science, but in all other fields as well, untrammelled by the dogma of the Church.

Protestantism has partly aided and partly impeded this social and intellectual development. It helped negatively by breaking the power of the Roman hierarchy over the minds of men and supporting the autonomy of national states. But in reality this only hastened a process, now practically completed, of the repudiation of the Church's political power. It was a Catholic Italy and a Catholic France that disestablished the Church in those countries, not a Protestant revolt. And it was a Catholic people, not a Protestant reformation that turned upon the Church in Mexico with a drastic program of disestablishment and even persecution. In fact, the Roman Church fares better and makes more progress today in Protestant England and America than in many so-called Catholic countries, because in those Protestant countries it is free from its own principle of autocratic control in the general life of the people, and stimulated by the free movement of thought which it itself did not encourage or permit in lands where it had dominance.

The role of Protestantism has been varied. The Protestant churches certainly did not arise as a movement for intellectual freedom; their obscurantist attitude toward philosophy and science has been as marked as has that of the Catholic church. Nor did they develop out of a passion for a Christian social or national ethic. The Calvinist theocracy was more Jewish than Christian and it represented not the attempt to embody a Christian ideal but the grim determination to rule human affairs by a divine authority. Those two things are radically different both in method and objective. The actual outcome of the theocratic venture was the final surrender of all responsibility of government to the secular political state. Calvinist Protestantism sanctioned the state as the instrument of God and preached "render unto Caesar the things that are Caesar's and unto God the things that are God's." Lutheran Protestantism had already accorded full autonomy to the state in temporal affairs. In effect, therefore, Protestantism has come very near to making itself irrelevant to the affairs of this earthly life. The national state has not been slow to enter into its heritage and has not only demanded of Christians all that they owe to Caesar, but has finally come to claim much that really belongs only to God, even the moral conscience itself.

A new conception of the role of Christianity in the common life is needed, and such a conception is finding expression today in what might be called liberal Christianity. I realize the peril in using the term "liberal" and perhaps had better make some definition of it. Indeed, a definition and description of liberal Protestantism is essential to this whole contention that Christianity has the answer to the world's need of a unifying faith. For that faith certainly is not the Catholic dogma nor the traditional Protestant creed, or variety of creeds. It is a new doctrine made possible by a more complete and unbiassed knowledge of history, and by free investigation into the origin and character of the scriptures, of the Church, and of the history and psychology of religion. This free movement of thought has not of itself created a true Christian doctrine; for many it has led to a purely naturalistic view of life. It is, in itself, only a method, but a method that true religion in the end must not only tolerate but support. What this free process of thought has done for us is to bring us back to that essentially ethical religion or religious ethics of Jesus and the early church, and to enable us to see therein the central truth and potency of Christianity. The whole prescientific and mythological world view of the early Christian era recedes into the background, becomes the relative historical form of the time, and allows the Christian doctrine of God and of man to stand forth with timeless validity. That doctrine gains an implementation it has never had before in the philosophy, psychology, and ethical theory of the modern world. It has itself powerfully contributed to the creation of these modern theories because of its lofty conception of man, even though that idea has too often been burdened and distorted by dogmatic theology.

The heart of liberal Christianity—its substance—is therefore that simple and persuasive teaching of Jesus which he expressed both in kindly deeds and in his heroic death, manifestations alike of the divine love that does good and suffers vicariously for sin; and in his effectual personal presence after the defeat of death. The method which is indispensable for the full work of this gospel is intellectual freedom from arbitrary and dogmatic control, and an essentially democratic process. Intellectual freedom and democracy, it must be repeated, are not of themselves the substance of faith; they need positive truth and reality as content and subject matter. But that content of the Christian gospel must have their aid if it is to be free to do its work of grace in the world. "You shall know the truth and the truth shall make you free" might well be taken as the principle of method by liberal Christianity. This method can be used confidently by those who really have faith in the Christian gospel; by those who believe that its truth can be demonstrated by free comparison with other teachings, and that its ideals will eventually find essential if not perfect embodiment in standards of personal morality and in the institutions of economic and political society.

This must plainly be seen not as a short-term enterprise, not as a five-year plan nor as a hundred-year plan. The outlook for free science and free religion is bad today; it may get much worse before it gets better. Christians today need both historic perspective and a confidence in eternal truth. There is not much point in treating the grand theme of world redemption on a small temporal scale. Even if the tendency to dictatorship and nationalism is relaxed no mature mind can take refuge either in a doctrine of evolutionary progress nor in utopianism. The sound Christian attitude is that the whole extent of history is to be a struggle of the spirit of God with the waywardness of man, and that the role of the Church in any generation and of the individual Christian is to strive to be true in testimony and life to the Christian ideal and to do all that can be done to influence the common life of men to that end.

This argument is based squarely upon the conviction that religion expresses the most fundamental insights, and releases the most creative and determinative forces in human life. Accordingly we confront here the issue between the great religious systems. We have surveyed the religions of the world according to the classification which is most significant to our purpose, and have discussed the principles by which various religions exercise control upon the practical life of men, or, it may be, renounce any responsibility for such control. If religion is the natural and necessary spiritual bond, then we must decide which religion has the capacity to fill that role in a world as diverse and difficult as ours.

In making this claim for Christianity we recognize the fact that there are many other forces contributing to this same end, and that there is, despite all selfishness and provincialism, a strong tendency in human nature toward widening fellowship. Education, art, political institutions, commerce, and all the common impulses of our nature contribute to the same end. But these forces are not strong enough; working against them are the rivalries and selfish interests of men, and so they need the undergirding of a powerful faith rooted in man's central conception and dedication. This is the function of religion.

Thus, while religion is not the sole force operating in human affairs, it is a profound and pervasive influence. What kind of influence it exerts is therefore of supreme practical importance. Each religion tends to create a certain effect, according to its own character. Each religion has typical results in so far as it gains control of the lives of men. That control is never complete and all religions are subject to periods of marked vigor and success, and also to periods of decay. Nevertheless, a religion that flourishes freely among any people over long periods of time will register its main idea and temper in the soul of the people. We look, then, to the typical results of the religions in lands where they have long been dominant.

HINDUISM

The most conspicuous work of Hinduism in human society is conservatism and fixity. But this is more than a matter of preserving unchanged the classifications of caste. That is the external fact. The inner attitude corresponding thereto is one of hopelessness. For this life caste is final, and that is a spiritual fact of the first magnitude. Underlying caste, and indeed, all of Hindu life, in the working of *karma*. Any man is in a particular caste because of the moral good and evil he has done in previous incarnations. His status, high or low, represents the exact degree of merit he has attained in past appearances upon the earth. It is piety to accept that status and condition and to increase his good karma during the present life so that in his next incarnation he will have a more fortunate position. But no essential improvement can be accomplished during one lifetime.

However, the prospects of an interminable series of rebirths during which the bad karma can be worked off and final deliverance achieved is profoundly depressing. This inexorable doctrine of karma represents the seriousness with which India has conceived the moral life. Despite its bad effects it merits our respect, even though it is a fundamental misconception of the nature of morality and the cosmic roots of man's ethical responsibility. Nevertheless, it has exercised a strange dominance over the Indian mind. There have been many revolts against it, the most impressive being Buddhism. But Buddhism, after centuries of widespread prevalence, finally disappeared

completely from India. Buddhism never really freed itself
from the karma doctrine. Other movements, and especially
the religions of salvation by grace, have opposed this doctrine
of karma, but its fundamental grip upon the religious mind
of India remains unbroken. Doubtless this is mainly due to
the connection of karma with the social system and the support it gives to a deep-rooted social conservatism. At any rate
its inevitable result is social stagnation and personal hopelessness. Religious doctrine not only confirms the *status quo* in
this life, but by its cosmic principle of karma makes the future
itself all but hopeless. What the religious man in India seeks
is escape from rebirth, but karma pushes that escape off to
a remote and uncertain future and wars against the doctrines
of grace by which men may be freed from its operation.

There are other factors working to the same end of stagnation and hopelessness in India, especially the climate and the
tremendous pressure of population upon the resources of the
land. A general temper is created that finds congenial expression in the religious doctrine, and the doctrine supports
that temper. But there have been and are many revolts against
the karma doctrine and many movements for social reform
despite climate and poverty. Today India is taking on new life
and hope and vigor. The old religion supported the old order;
a new religious spirit and idea are needed to give spiritual
power for the new day.

ISLAM

Islam is in many ways a very different religion from
Hinduism. It is militantly monotheistic and makes more of
divine sovereignty than does any other religion. It has been
the faith of vigorous races living under all sorts of climatic

conditions. Prosperity and plenty have been the lot of Moslem peoples as well as poverty. The history of Islam does not reveal a languid race geographically isolated and turned inward for spiritual release from the hard realities of life. Moslems have ranged free and by conquest and commerce have extended the faith among many peoples.

Yet, with all this evidence of vigor, Moslem doctrine has one social result which is not so very different from that of Hinduism. Islam, too, has a principle that paralyzes personal effort and tends to social stagnation. It is the belief in fatalism. The unrelieved doctrine of divine sovereignty has issued in this idea. All that happens is decreed by God. All the details of each man's life are fixed by the arbitrary will of Allah. What can man do? If misfortune comes, it is *kismet*. Man must accept it. Vigorous action on the part of the individual or society to change the course of events, remove evils and make things better, runs counter to the idea that God has determined all things. To seek to change the course of events is both futile and impious. So a devout Moslem who has been greatly impressed by the person and teachings of Jesus, expressed the basic Moslem idea when he said that since war is in the world, though it is a great evil, it must be here by God's will and we must make no effort to stop it. And so with all evils.

Being a totalitarian religion, Islam has been unusually resistant to outside ideas. For four hundred years the blight of this fatalistic conception has made Moslem civilization backward, both socially and intellectually. Today Turkey, an overwhelmingly Moslem country, has found it necessary to bar all religious ideas from education and social and political life in her program of progress and modernization. That is one way to deal with Moslem conservatism. It means a rejection of religion and the cultivation of a secular society. Another attack upon the old order comes from liberal Moslem theologians, of which there are all too few. Sir Mohammed Iqbal, one of the ablest and most outspoken of them, approves the course of Turkey and calls for a complete reconstruction of Moslem theology in the light of western science and philosophy.[1] Particularly does he attack the idea of fatalism. In an illuminating discussion of the question of divine sovereignty which I heartily commend to Christian students for its intrinsic worth, he makes a distinction between divine rule by a fixed diagrammatic decree and rule by a non-prescriptive purpose. He makes a valuable contribution to religious thinking in this matter. If Moslems generally should accept his interpretation it would certainly work a revolution in their religious doctrine. Of this, however, there now seems little likelihood. The all-absorbing, all-dominating character of Islam, together with this idea of fatalism, makes of it a supremely reactionary force in human affairs.

BUDDHISM

Crossing the China-Manchukuo border at Shankaikwan, I was interviewed by an Englishman whose card declared him to be the general manager of the Manchukuo State Railways. He said he was getting news items for a Tientsin newspaper. This rather humble task being performed by one with such a high title seemed to indicate that the bearer of it was in effect a "front" for the Japanese owners, whose duty was to find out all he could about foreigners going into China. At any rate, he asked me why I was going to China. I told him

[1] *Reconstruction of Religious Thought in Islam.*

that one of my purposes was to find out, if I could, the net value to China of a hundred years of Christian missionary work. That seemed to call for comment, and he gave it in a breezy manner somewhat as follows: "If that is what you are after, I'd advise you to send your missionaries home as soon as you can and leave it to Buddha."

Well, why not leave China to Buddha? That goes to the heart of our present inquiry. What has been and what is now the effect of Buddhism on Chinese civilization? Buddhism entered China in the first century of our era. It has often had imperial support and favor. It has developed Chinese sects and scriptures and has produced saints and philosophers. It, alone, of the great world religions has had time and opportunity to register its distinctive effects on the character of Chinese life. Just now, it is true, Buddhism is decadent in China. In contrast to the vigor of Japanese Buddhism it appears impotent and irrelevant to the moral needs of modern China. In the Western Hills a few miles out of Peiping is a Buddhist temple, the Wu Fu Ssu, and the central object in that temple is a great golden figure of the Buddha lying with the head resting upon the palm of one hand, asleep. This might be taken as a symbol of Buddhism in China today.

But it has not always been so. Buddhism has had great influence in China. It has affected but did not furnish the constructive form of ethics in China. That has been the work of Confucianism. However, the two systems do not seem to have been in serious conflict. Possibly that is due to the fact that Confucianism is primarily an ethical system with no ambition for cosmic speculation, while Buddhism has been a speculative philosophy with little concern for practical ethics.

The real influence of Buddhism appears in two tendencies

which are inherent in its doctrine, viz., individualism and quietism. The only social form created by Buddhism is the sangam, the fellowship of monks. This, however, is a fellowship of retirement from the world, and the way of deliverance for all, even for the monk, is not in the fellowship but in the individual achievement of each one apart from his fellows. It is in private meditation, not in any common act of service or even of worship that salvation is attained. The social religion of China is the family cult with its worship of ancestors and observance of the annual festivals.

This means that Buddhism has contributed powerfully to the development of that individualism which is one of the most marked traits of Chinese life. In China both foreigners and Chinese tell one that individualism is one of China's greatest elements of weakness. A Christian pastor in Tientsin told me that and expressed it by this striking comparison: "One Chinese is equal to one Japanese or one American, but ten Chinese are not equal to ten Japanese or ten Americans." He then went on to say that one of the most important things Christianity is doing for China is to teach Chinese the value of cooperation.

However, the whole blame for Chinese individualism cannot be laid upon Buddhism. Natural human selfishness and the limiting of social responsibility to the large family both work to the same end. But it seems perfectly clear that in so far as it has affected the general outlook Buddhism has given support to this tendency and has offered no opposition to it; indeed, that its whole conception of life has undergirded Chinese individualism with a metaphysical and a religious ideal.

Being a religion of inaction, Buddhism has furnished Chinese life with no impulse to betterment. It is said in China that when a general is defeated in battle or when a politician fails in public life he retires to a monastery and becomes a Buddhist monk. Buddhism has become the true religion of escape from reality; indeed, it is that in principle. While it is good to find in religion a haven of refuge, yet to have as essential religious doctrine the conviction that all action in society is futile and vain means that the energies of religious devotion are withdrawn from the common life. The world must go its secular way while the individual finds salvation in a quietistic faith. Not work but meditation opens the way to deliverance. This is in sharp contrast to the temper of another religion whose founder said "my Father worketh even until now, and I work," and "we must work the works of him who sent me while it is yet day," and many other similar things.

Why not leave China to Buddha? The answer in 1935 and now is found in China's transition from individualism to co-operative effort and from quietism to intense activity. Buddha has no positive support for a cooperative, dynamic, and progressive society. Its effect on civilization as seen in China is to encourage individualism and inaction. But now China has entered upon a period of unprecedented activity in which a premium is placed upon social responsibility and cooperation.

This brief survey of the effects of three great non-Christian religions on civilization does not claim to tell the whole story of those religions. But our point is that the fundamental characteristic of any religion shows itself in a definite influence upon human affairs: Hinduism supports a static and unprogressive society because of its doctrine of karma; Islam is reactionary and productive of moral inertia because of the fatalism which is in turn the natural fruit of an over-simplified idea of divine sovereignty; and Buddhism, being in principle individualistic and quietistic, gives support to the individualism and social irresponsibility which have been the curse of China. In some cases these social results go along with other influences to determine the character of a people; in other cases they contend with those other forces. In India Hinduism has absorbed and subdued many revolts against both caste and karma. Certainly the fatalism of Islam has been opposed by the vigor of many races, and today in Turkey a tide of adverse purposes has routed it completely. Turkey turns toward Europe, progress, and man's power to do something for himself.

We should view Christianity in the same way as that in which we have considered these other religions. Realizing that in the places where it has prevailed many other forces have shared in creating the character of civilization, at the same time we may look for the peculiar contribution Christianity has made to the total result. There is a long history in regard to Christendom itself, and more than a century of missionary expansion in the modern period gives us concrete evidence of the effect of Christianity when its influence is at work in the non-Christian world.

No false effort to be tolerant should prevent our frank recognition that there are some forms of organized Christianity which effectually frustrate the vital principle and ideal of the gospel. Historically, Christianity has all too often been an institution and a rite symbolically Christian, but in thought and spiritual attitude as pagan as the non-Christians it has sought to evangelize. Idolatry, polytheism, and gross superstition have prevailed and still do prevail in areas where Eastern Orthodox and Roman Catholic Christianity have long been dominant. There the ethical dynamic and spiritual freedom which are of the essence of a true Christianity are all but lost. This is not to say that there are not good works and saintly souls in such areas, but that the general influence upon the common life is not productive of enlightenment, progress, or high ethical achievement. And this is due directly to a misconception and practical misinterpretation of Christianity.

In too large measure the Protestant forms of Christianity also have been so much concerned with an essentially doctrinal and ecclesiastical kind of religion that a dubious contribution has been made to the common life. And yet a striking characteristic of the Protestant mission in the last century has been the emergence of that essential humanism which so dominates the mind and teaching of Jesus. Even sects intensely devoted to a dogmatic system and to an other-worldly idea of salvation have actually exerted a strong stimulus to all forms of intellectual, physical, and social improvement. We think of the missionaries who went to Hawaii over a hundred years ago as stern, doctrinally minded devotees concerned solely about the future life. And they were all that, excepting the "solely." As a matter of fact many of them were not ordained men but printers, carpenters and farmers, and their conception of their task has an amazingly modern sound, as witness the following extract from the Minutes of the Eleventh Annual Meeting of the American Board:

The passage having been engaged, and other preparatory arrangements made, the mission family assembled in Boston, on the 12th of October (1819). It consisted of twenty-two persons, and presented a most interesting collection, rarely if ever surpassed on a similar occasion. The Rev. Messrs. Bingham and Thurston had been ordained as ministers of the Gospel. Mr. Daniel Chamberlain, of Brookfield, Mass., a farmer in the prime of life, who, by his own industry and good management, was placed in very eligible worldly circumstances; Dr. Thomas Holman, who had just finished his education for the practice of medicine; Mr. Samuel Whitney, a student in Yale College, capable of being employed as a catechist, schoolmaster, or mechanic; Mr. Samuel Ruggles, a catechist and schoolmaster; and Mr. Elisha Loomis, a printer, having previously offered themselves for this service and been accepted, went forth desirous of carrying the arts of civilized communities, as well as the blessing of the Gospel.

Many of us lament the large percentage of fundamentalist missionaries in the Orient today—overlooking the fact that it corresponds roughly to the predominance of fundamentalist churches in our own country—but there is some cause for comfort in the fact that even strongly conservative bodies are, increasingly, channels for the real spiritual and ethical potency of the gospel.

The American ambassador to China, the Honorable Nelson T. Johnson, pointed out to me, in an interview at Peiping, some of the constructive influences of Protestant Christianity already observable in Chinese life. I mention two which seem peculiarly important as indicating the logical results of the Christian idea. First, by the translation of the Bible into Mandarin, the spoken language of the common people, a strong impulse was given to the creation of a literature that all could read and also to the rapid extension of literacy. As a result, Chinese leaders in all realms have today a literary vehicle of communication with a rapidly growing constituency. The new unity and strength of China could not have been achieved without this common written language. The other thing done by the Protestant missionary, and especially the American missionary, has been to teach organization to the Chinese. China has been helpless before the forces of the modern world because of her rank individualism and the dominance of the large family. But the missionary has given China a century of training in organization. He has organized churches, schools, hospitals, flood and famine relief, rural reconstruction, and other enterprises. And everything he has organized has had two salutary results. It has given a visible demonstration of the power of organization, and it has given practical training in organization to all who have had part in it. In all this there has been the implanting of the spirit and attitude of cooperation, as the Tientsin pastor said, which has changed the Chinese inwardly as well as outwardly. China still has far to go, but she is well on her way, and not even war and Japanese aggression can suppress the new forces now at work.

What needs to be pointed out here is that these by-products, for such they are, of Protestant Christianity are natural fruits of the Christian idea. It is true that Christian missionaries did not go to China to help create a literary medium for the common man, nor to teach the Chinese organization. These are not exclusively Christian nor are they by any means always used for Christian ends. But it is not by chance, nor purely incidentally, that such works are done by Protestant missionaries. They grow out of a conception of the Christian faith and life. One of the two main principles of the Protestant Reformation is the right of private interpretation of the scriptures. Not alone the clergy but the layman as well is entitled to direct access to the chief literary sources of the Christian faith. Practically, this means that each one must be able and free to read the Bible for himself. It is material, therefore, to the purpose of the Protestant missionary that prospective converts be taught to read.

As a matter of fact, this basic assumption of the intellectual and moral responsibility of the individual Christian is the original impulse toward general education in Protestantism and goes far to explain some differences between Catholic and Protestant countries. The Protestant Christian must have intelligence in religion because he has ultimate responsibility. But once throw that emphasis upon the value of education and there is no point at which the process can be stopped. The full development of all powers of mind and all branches of knowledge is already implied.

Similarly, the training in organization is a direct and logical outcome both of the responsibility for practical moral conduct which Protestantism lays upon the individual, and also of the fundamental Christian impulse to fellowship. If fellowship is to be more than a sentiment it means that men must work together for the common good. Because of this Christianity is known, and truly known, in the Orient as the religion of activity. It is much more than that, of course, but it is always that, and not because of the vigorous character of the American and European peoples who send missionaries, but because of the insistent teaching and example of Jesus and his early disciples.

The natural effects of Christianity upon civilization are (1) an ethical impulse which expresses itself not merely in zeal for personal morality, but also in developing forms of human service and a profound concern for human welfare; (2) a stimulus to education and the full development of intellectual and moral powers; and (3) the encouragement of social responsibility and cooperative effort for the general improvement of human life. These actually are in varying measure the results of Protestant Christianity in the Orient today. Nowhere are they as pure and complete as they might be. The resistance of an old order and attitude, the natural inertia and selfishness of men, and the imperfect expression of these impulses both by missionaries and by the native Church, all make them less potent than they ought to be and might be. But there is no question that these are the true effects of Christianity wherever it has a fair chance over a reasonable period of time, and is not too much obstructed by false and irrelevant elements.

Here is the great responsibility of liberal Christianity. It is free from the dogmatisms of both Catholic and fundamentalist Protestant churches. It is free to serve these true Christian objectives in the spiritual, moral, and cultural life of men. It has won its freedom by the Protestant appeal to individual liberty of mind and conscience; now it must justify that freedom by carrying the full meaning of Christianity as a gospel of personal salvation and of human service and social regeneration. It must recognize the full power and duty of the Christian Church to the civilized life of man.

CHAPTER V

The Religious Character of the World Mission

THE CHRISTIAN WORLD MISSION IS ESSENTIALLY A RELIGIOUS enterprise. Christianity itself is a religion; its potency in human affairs springs from its religious faith and dynamic. Its goal is nothing less than the complete redemption of human life from fear to confidence, from strife to fellowship, from hate to love. The secure ground of the Christian effort toward this goal is the revelation of God's purpose to attain it. This is primarily God's enterprise, not ours. We follow His leadership made human and explicit in the person of Jesus Christ. The Christian has a gospel which he has received and which he proclaims—the good news of this great purpose of God for man. Our faith, our hopes for man, our sense of mission, all rest upon this divine initiative, and we are moved by the impulse to do God's will and work with Him toward the realization of His purpose.

The more Christian we are in our religion and the more religious we are in our Christianity the more are we possessed by enthusiasm for the world mission. I say "the more Christian we are in our religion" because there is much earnest religion that is only partially Christian. Much religion in the churches today is a self-centered interest in personal culture and well-being, untouched by any Christian concern for those people either on the other side of the world or on the other side of the railroad tracks. There have been long periods in the history of the Church when its energies were absorbed in doctrinal matters and in the more or less political interests of the Church as an institution, and no compulsion was felt to carry either the news or the works of God's purpose to other men. I say "the more religious we are in our Christianity" because the zeal for such a thankless and far-flung task as that of Christian missions can only be created and sustained when we are moved by the large vision of a divine purpose and the passion of a divine love. So long as the objectives of our Christianity are limited to the world of our own immediate interest and experience we are likely to remain pretty parochial in our enthusiasms. Religious faith releases both thought and imagination and stirs men to living on a grand scale. Some of the humbler people of our communities—those who serve God in sects with narrow intellectual outlook and in the forms of outworn doctrine—are really thinking more in cosmic terms and adjusting their actual living more to the scheme of a grand sweep of history, than are most of the cultured members of our liberal churches. They do it because they are viewing human life and history as the scene of God's activity and they humbly seek to join themselves to the really significant thing that is going on in the world. They are fundamentally right in this even though some of their ideas and perhaps methods are sadly wrong.

Whatever the degree of our enlightenment, our original impulse in the Christian mission is religious. It is God's work we seek to do; it is His purpose we seek to serve. This is the point of difference between the Christian missionary in any area of activity and the secular idealist. There is much idealism in the world today, and many groups and movements are working to better the lot of man on the earth. In many respects these movements put organized religion to shame, especially the organized Christian Church which has been unfaithful to its mandate from Christ to concern itself with the human needs and welfare of men. In practice the Christian finds in these efforts for human betterment an activity in which he can cooperate. We work for peace, for social justice, for health and the abolition of poverty, side by side with many who do not recognize the religious basis of our life. In fact, there are a great many who cannot believe that religion has anything to do with their human causes. In India I talked for two hours with a worker of the Self Respect movement trying to get him to admit that *some* people *might* be moved to social service and reform by their religious faith—but without success. The most he would say was that he and his fellows were willing to work with people who believed in religion. He claimed that the impulse to human service had nothing to do with religion but stood on its own feet, as it were, and entirely human feet at that. Too often and with too much justification, social idealists look upon organized religion and even religious belief as obstacles to the realization of their ideals.

There is, however, a difference between secular social idealism and the impulse of the Christian to serve his fellow man. Perhaps the simplest way to express that difference is to say that the former depends upon the will of man, and the latter upon the will of God. The ideals themselves may be very much alike, and in some respects identical. And ideals are made and operate in the same way. We have changed the meaning of "ideal" in recent years under the influence of a pragmatic philosophy, but some of the moral quality and prestige of the older platonic meaning still cling to it. In the older sense of the term the ideal was thought of as a perfect and eternal form which culminated in the Idea of the Good.

Essentially all idealism was moral idealism because all ideals were good. An ideal was something already there in a higher order of being, and by our thinking or perhaps by our faith we found it; having been discovered, it became the goal for our faithful effort.

Now secular social idealism, following the pragmatic philosophy, does not use the term "ideal" in that meaning at all. For it the ideal is just an idea constructed by the human mind to represent what it considers a more perfect or more satisfactory condition of life. It represents a purely human objective for effort because it is a purely human conception of something better. Manifestly this kind of ideal is not a pre-existing reality in a higher order of being to which man can penetrate by his rational thought, or which he may perceive by the intuition of faith. Nor can it claim to be perfect. The mind that makes it is not perfect, and indeed our ideals change so often that we would be most indiscreet if we should ever claim perfection for the last construction of an ideal of any kind. As a matter of fact, that is what many social dogmatists actually do; it is the vice and the error of utopianism. Being man's mental construction representing something better than he now enjoys, the ideal is, of course, cast in terms, more or less, of his present need. A hungry man's ideal will certainly have a lot to do with a plentiful food supply; a Marie Curie's ideal will be made up of laboratories and technical apparatus and freedom to use them. This kind of ideal is relative to the conscious need and desire of men. It may even be morally bad. There are many people who consider the ideal of Adolf Hitler lacking in moral goodness, but there is no doubt that he has the ideal, and that it is stirring millions of Germans to passionate effort.

The old idealism has gone; Christianity trusted too much to it, not understanding its defects. The new idealism of the secular mind is no less a false basis for human faith and living. The ideal *per se* is neither divine, moral, nor perfect: it is simply the mental pattern of a humanly desired goal with a more or less detailed indication of the means for attaining that goal. Now this technique of creating and following ideals is the specific way by which rational men must work at the task of improving human life. It is definitely more hopeful than the older habit of cherishing as an ideal a real or mythological past. To have discovered what ideals are and what they are good for is a great gain in method. But the secular idealist must give up his illicit smuggling of a certain divine and moral quality for his ideal, because with the passing of the platonic Idea that quality has also ceased to be inherent in the ideal as such. Secular idealism is thrown back for its moral claims upon the desires and the wills of men, and these are themselves notoriously in need of rectification from a higher source.

The Christian sense of mission in life, that which moves him to human service of any kind, is the conviction that God has made known His will and purpose in Christ, and that the goal of human life is the fulfilment of God's will and the positive joy in fellowship with God and with men which will be found thereby. The good which the Christian seeks for himself and for others cannot be found in some perfect ideal pattern to be apprehended by mental effort or discerned by faith, but it is to be discovered and achieved as men change their hearts and wills to conform to the divine purpose. There is no use quarreling with the non-religious idealist because he is not religious, but this difference should be made clear. The secular idealist is trying to realize his own will and desire; the Christian is trying to discover and to do the will of God, and to learn how to desire aright. In this religion serves the Christian and especially the norm and spirit that he finds in Christ. He has the full assurance that through spiritual communion and devotion he can find not alone increasing indication of the divine purpose as a vital experience, but also the power and courage to follow it.

The Christian mission is not an international charity. In effect it has been looked upon as such, and that has done great disservice to the cause of Christian missions. There has been a great deal of superficial evidence to indicate that it is essentially a world program of humanitarian service. There is hardly any kind of human service that has not been performed by missionaries, and this service is given, in large measure, to peoples who do not know how to help themselves and who lack both the education and the means to do it. Christian missionaries have taken scientific medicine, education, knowledge of diet, and sanitation to all parts of the earth. They have inaugurated a new regime in these matters in the great old civilizations of the Orient as well as among peoples relatively low in the scale of culture. There is an enormous number of individuals who have benefited in health and education through institutions largely supported by money given for missions. Read the annual report of any mission board and you will find figures mounting into the hundreds of thousands. It is true that these institutions tend to become self-supporting, especially the hospitals, but millions of dollars went into their founding and development, and a large proportion of the missionary dollar still goes to support them.

In addition to the maintenance of the institutional work

which is an integral part of their program, missionaries have always been leaders in actual relief and charitable work. Flood and famine relief in China was first organized and carried on by missionaries. In the fall of 1935 when I was in China this work had been turned over to a responsible agency of the Chinese Government, but even then missionaries were giving their aid at key points in administration of the relief program. There was a period after the war when the whole American Board staff in the Near East was engaged in the Near East Relief, the greatest international organized charity ever carried on in history. These are large and well-known enterprises, but, aside from such large-scale efforts, an incalculable amount of direct service to human need has been done by missionaries. Sometimes this has been a cause for bitter protest by nationals not in sympathy with Christianity. They have charged the missionaries with "buying" converts, and from the point of view of the missionary himself it has been something of a liability because it has brought many "rice Christians" into the Church. Nevertheless, the impulse of human sympathy which prompts this service is essentially Christian, and, despite all the problems that it creates, it was inevitable that it should be done. "Whoso hath the world's goods, and beholdeth his brother in need, and shutteth up his compassion from him, how doth the love of God abide in him."[1]

Missionaries are notorious for the simplicity and frugality of their standards of living and the resources of mission boards are never adequate to the needs pressing upon them, but this is true when measured by the standards and resources of our own country. To the average man in the Orient or in

[1] I John 3:17.

Africa the mission and the missionary are symbols of wealth. Actually they do come from a land where wealth and general standards of living are far above those of the people with whom they work. A fairly successful man in India will not have the income or advantages of an ordinary workman with a steady job in America. An incidental aspect of the Christian mission, due to the great disparity in wealth between the West and the East, is this aspect of charity. But it is only incidental. There are many situations in which missionaries serve individuals and groups far more prosperous than they themselves are, and who are in no need of charity. From the beginning, the Christian Church in Japan has included many from the upper middle class. No question of charity has been involved; indeed, much charity has been done by Japanese Christians themselves. Yet the missionary has had a full program of his essential religious work to do. In China I met a group of business and professional people in the home of a missionary. They were by no means objects of charity; some of them arrived in good automobiles driven by their chauffeurs. But there seemed to be in that group a more definite consciousness of need for the help of the missionary than there was among humbler groups. It was help of a religious character they were seeking—and getting. The moral issues of life, both personal and national, weighed heavily upon them, and they were seeking in Christianity a solution to those issues.

If Christianity had only charity for the poor, but no strong, clear word of faith and hope for these leaders of Chinese society and others like them, it would indeed be but a poor and futile thing. But Christianity has that word of faith and hope and courage, because it is a religion. It is, indeed, a eligion which prompts the humblest service to human need, but it is also a religion which brings to the soul of man an assurance of divine love and companionship and makes the struggle of life meaningful in the light of the divine purpose. Only a pitifully low conception of human life can represent men as being sufficiently served when they are put in the way of getting health for their bodies and enough education to make a living. Christianity has no such conception of man; it would be utterly false to its own teaching and the Christ it serves were it not passionately concerned to make every man aware of himself, in whatever state of health and wealth, as an object of God's love and as a member of the Kingdom of God. That is the religious purpose of the Christian mission. "Seek ye first his kingdom and his righteousness, and all these things shall be added unto you." It is the fundamental faith of Christianity that all good things in human life are ultimately to be achieved through a primary discovery and performance of God's will. That includes the good things of the spirit which are too often lacking when men have enough and to spare of other things; indeed, which seem to be endangered by the very possession in too great abundance of material things.

While, therefore, the Christian mission has given itself freely to works of charity on a large scale and in innumerable small ways as an essential expression of human sympathy, its central motive goes far deeper and concerns the relation of men to God and the inner transformation of life which true religion brings. The Christian is not content until he has made available to those whom he serves the full knowledge and grace of God by which he himself lives. He is not willing to give some of the lesser things and withhold the greater. He

wants to make God fully known and to bring into the fellowship of His kingdom every one who will receive Him. He
does not want forever to sit at the table and provide crumbs
for hungry bodies; he wants all who will to sit at the same
table and have an equal part in the knowledge and fellowship
of God.

But we have educated the Church too much to think of
the Christian mission in terms of a world-wide charity. It has
been an easy thing to do. Reacting from a barren, dogmatic
type of religion the Protestant churches have for a generation
or more been trying to make religion real in the sense of making it practical. Practical religion has meant, first, personal
morality, then, social service, and, more recently, the social
gospel. The elementary services of health and education have
bulked large in this interest in practical religion, and the
easiest way to interest the members of our churches in missionary work has been to tell them of such work on the
mission field. It is remarkable that the general run of church
members do not feel equally the importance of making religion real in the sense of inner change and the richness of
a personal experience of God. The idea that the supreme
achievement of religion is the inner peace and power and
victory which Christ makes possible, does not seem sufficiently
to have impressed Christians generally. It is to be feared that
in "liberal" churches more than in others the outward results
of religion have been more highly prized than the intrinsic
spiritual value of religious experience itself. It is time we re-
cover from this swing to the extrovert extreme and begin
to realize that there is no true profit to any man if he gain
the whole world and lose his own soul, and that religion is

reeminently a way of the soul in its supreme experience of
nding God and being found by Him.

This appeal to the churches for support of missions on the
asis of their humanitarian works has brought large response.
And it is a true Christian impulse that prompts church mem-
ers to support such work. The human sympathy that is not
imited to family or class or nation is one of the finest and
most authentic notes in Christian character. But it becomes
uperficial when it is separated from the more fundamental
eligious faith of Christianity. Taken by itself it is a false and
nstable basis for the Christian mission. Because it has been
aken that way there has arisen a certain type of objection to
he foreign mission, expressed something like this: "Why
hould we send money and missionaries to other countries
when there is so much poverty and need in our own country?
Charity should begin at home." Yes, charity should begin at
nome although even charity should never stop there. But the
Christian mission to non-Christian countries is not a charity.
Such charity as is done is always secondary; our primary
purpose is to give to the people of those countries the Christian faith in its fullness. It is not because the people are poor
or sick in body that the missionary goes to them, but because
they do not know God and because they, like us, need the
moral and spiritual salvation that is made possible by Christ.
The prosperous and healthy in body need that salvation as
much as the poor, sometimes more than they. A rich and
powerful sinner is a more dangerous person both to himself
and to others than a sinner among the more humble. Such
a person is often more definitely a damned soul than those
about him. The privileged as well as the under-privileged
have sinned and come short of the glory of God and need

the gospel of repentance. High and low need Christ and need to learn of him the way into the Kingdom of God. It is the primary and permanent work of the Christian Church to make him and his way known and to impart to men the motivation which will produce throughout the whole range of human life the fruits of his Kingdom.

Missionaries and mission board secretaries have been partly to blame for this misconception of the Christian mission. We have told people those things in which we knew they would be interested and which would make obvious the useful character of missionary work. Then there has been during the past generation a great development of institutional work. At least up to the time of the depression there was a continuous expansion of schools and hospitals, and of the buildings and equipment for their use. Many people of means when making large gifts insist that those gifts be used for the construction of buildings. Assuredly there is an unlimited need for schools and hospitals. Even in our own country with its great endowed universities and colleges there are constant appeals to the alumni for more funds, to say nothing of the needs of tax-supported institutions. No one can say that the relatively small amount that has been put into mission schools and hospitals has not been urgently needed. But this very expansion of the visible equipment of the missions has focussed attention upon visible results, and has encouraged the belief that the major work is health and education.

There is, however, a more deep-lying and disturbing reason for this emphasis upon what might be called, without disparagement, the secular character of Christian missions, that is, an essential loss of conviction of the real importance of religion. We have gone through a period—there are signs that we are nearly *through* it—in which many, both in the pulpit and in the pew, have been basically uncertain in their religious belief. This has been due not merely to a questioning of old religious formulas and doctrines, but to something deeper—to a decline of faith in the objective reality of God and the spiritual ends which are the substance of religious faith. For many, religion has not rested squarely upon its own foundation of the reality of God and the supreme importance of man's relation to Him; to find justification for its place in human life it must be made a sanction for morality and a motivation for social usefulness. It is obvious that that is the end of religion, for if religion has no authority or truth in its own right it speedily becomes but a superstitious encumbrance upon the cause of human service. Men of clear mind and honest hearts will simply drop it by the wayside while they go about the thing that is real and rests upon its own inherent worth.

But the Church has not been able simply to discard religion. It has sought to keep it by re-defining it in terms of humanitarian enthusiasm. Churches, strangely enough, have had zeal for the teaching of scientific truth to non-Christians far beyond their interest in teaching Christian truth to them. There are still many who make a virtue of their unwillingness to win men from their old religions to the Christian faith. It has seemed obviously worth while to teach scientific knowledge, but doubtful at the best whether there were any real good done by teaching the Christian religion. This attitude is a direct menace to the very continuance of religion. It is a thoroughly irrational and contradictory situation that the one institution in human life whose chief concern is religion, the Church, should even entertain the idea that the validity of its religious service to mankind is doubtful and if carried on at all must be justified by other services whose worth is taken for granted. And yet the Church has been very deeply influenced by just such an attitude. What has made it possible?

Aside from the religious skepticism which has already been mentioned, there is one widespread error which, more than any other thing in the thought of church people, has been responsible for the lack of zeal on the part of the Church for the propagation of the Christian faith. It may be stated somewhat like this: "Religions differ superficially in many ways but when we get down to their fundamental ideas they all teach about the same things." This is usually said with an air of intellectual superiority. It conveys the impression that the one who says it has a wider range of knowledge and a more unbiassed mind than others. It seems to reflect a large tolerance. But the amazing thing is that it is usually said by those who know almost nothing about the great religions of the world. It must be said, in all kindness, that those who make such a statement speak not out of knowledge but out of ignorance.

Why do people say that sort of thing? Very few of them know anything at all about the non-Christian religions. I have frequently heard fairly well-informed and educated people ask questions, or make remarks in which, for example, there is a hopeless confusion of Buddhism and Islam—and it would be hard to find two religions more different. For that matter, there is a widespread ignorance as to what Christianity is. If a tenth of the energy and effort had gone into the study of Christianity that has gone into any one of a number of secular subjects, there would be a beginning at least of knowledge of what it is and what its teachings and principles are. Some of this ignorance about religion is due to the fact that not too well-informed preachers and others have in the past caricatured non-Christian religions in order to condemn them, and have at the same time made claims of absolute truth for Christianity as interpreted in terms of narrow, sectarian dogma. I suppose there are still many persons going through the reaction from that attitude, but religion is too important and Christian truth is too vital a need to human life to let it go at that. One dogmatism does not justify another, and the spiritual life and faith of men suffer while this intellectual pendulum swings from one pole to the other.

As a matter of fact, it is precisely when we get down to the really basic ideas, to the regulative principles and conceptions of the various religions, that we find fundamental differences. Superficially religions look very much alike. If one without any special knowledge of religious ways should go successively into a Buddhist temple, an Eastern Orthodox Church, and a Roman Catholic Church, and observe the services, one would find it very easy to believe that they are but variations in the practices of the same religion. There would be in all robed priests, processions, idols or objects of veneration, chants, incense, and other symbolic acts. These are the externals of religion. But inquire into the meaning of these things, into the beliefs and ideas that lie back of them, and one would find radical differences. To go further and visit a Moslem mosque and a Protestant Christian church one would find not even superficial resemblances, and would discover even more radical differences in idea.

There are in fact as great differences between religions as there are between forms and principles of government. There is a real difference between a fascist state and a true constitutional monarchy. Superficially they are alike in many things.

A foreigner might go about in Germany, buy what he wanted, ask a traffic officer for directions, ride on the railways, see the opera, tour the country in his automobile, and get along about as he would in England. In both countries, if he were 'an American, he might be a bit annoyed when he registered at a hotel because he had to fill out a report for the police. Superficially he would find the two countries very much the same. He would see military pomp in the changing of the guard at Buckingham Palace and an exceedingly warlike lot of statues and memorials in St. Paul's, and there would be sufficient evidence in Germany that the Reich has an army. But the traveler would not even have to go first to the Reichstag and then to the House of Parliament to discover that the two countries are governed on very different principles. Further inquiry would show that those differences are real and have tremendous practical implications.

The same is true of religions. In the preceding chapters I have tried to point out some of the more obviously important differences, especially as they affect the organized life of societies. These differences have their roots in even deeper divergences in conceptions of God, of man, and of human destiny. This is not to say that one religion is wholly true and all others vicious and false. Religions in their fundamental patterns of thought are answers to ultimate questions about the nature of existence and the true meaning of the universe and of human life. They all have spiritual and moral disciplines that are of value to earnest believers. They all express a consciousness of the divine and are evidences of the self-revelation of God. In the advanced religions there are profound speculations upon the nature of spiritual reality and lofty conceptions of the moral life. They represent traditions of spiritual exploration and discovery and the high attainment of men who have known God in varying degrees.

But there are crucial points at which they differ and vital points at which they fail. Orthodox Hinduism is a strict ☩ monism; in place of a personal God there is an impersonal absolute. Islam is a strict monotheism; its God is a personal but arbitrary sovereign. Mahayana Buddhism has many gods, as does popular Hinduism. Islam is a totalitarian religion; it would control all the affairs of human life by religious law. Buddhism is a way of individual salvation which renounces all responsibility for the mundane life of men except to teach them how eventually to escape it.[2] These are differences at least as great as those between democracy and fascism in politics. It is true that our common nature and the compromises with principle which run through all human life tend to minimize the differences. England and America are not wholly democratic; nor has Germany completely conformed to the Nazi ideal. Many intellectual, cultural, and social influences play upon people and modify the rigorous expression of the religious principle, but the radical differences are there and in so far as religion does influence life the results are different in the different religious systems. There are many nominal followers of all religions, including Christianity, who know little of the teachings of their religion and care less about following them. Even these people, however, are profoundly affected by the major ideas and attitudes of the religious faith which condition the life around them.

The fundamental reason for the Christian world mission lies

[2] F. Harold Smith, *The Elements of Comparative Theology* (London, Duckworth), gives in brief compass and non-technical language a clear treatment of the vital differences in the basic ideas of the world's main religions.

in the fact that Christianity has the clearest revelation of God's will and nature. It represents the great historic discovery of religious truth which came after centuries of progress in the Hebrew prophetic line and found full expression in the experience and life of Jesus Christ. This is a truth both of ideas and of personal embodiment. It includes and transcends all that is true in other religions. Is that bigotry and intolerance? I think not. It is not intolerant to say that Newtonian physics includes and transcends all that is true in the various schools of science that preceded Isaac Newton, nor that the same is true of the modern physics which includes and transcends all that is true in Newtonian physics. A real discovery of truth does not invalidate all the knowledge that men have had before it, but it does reorient it and give it new meanings; some things are of course definitely proved false. This is as true in religion as it is in science. Even in modern physics there are many unanswered questions, but the answers when found will be consistent with some fundamental truths already known. There are plenty of unanswered questions in religion, but we need not fear that the final answers Jesus gave to some of them will ever be challenged. That God is both righteousness and love; that man can turn to Him in penitence and faith and find salvation; that love even for one's enemies is right, and that vicarious suffering by God and man is the way by which the world is saved from its sin, that God wills a human society in which good-will is the bond of fellowship—these are fundamental truths that have emerged through the Judeo-Christian religious tradition and which find personal embodiment in the historic Jesus. We shall in varying degrees perceive their implications and realize them in our personal and social life, but there is nothing true that will invalidate them.

To be sure, various parts of this doctrine are found in other religions. In some respects non-Christian teachings approach very near to the Christian; in other points they go in the opposite direction. All too often the light of truth is dimmed in Christian churches by irrelevant ideas and practices and sometimes it is completely obscured. There are thus always two tasks before the Church: first, to purify its understanding and the expression of its own doctrine; and second, to teach that doctrine to others. As a matter of fact one of the most effective stimuli to do the first is the serious endeavor to do the second. We discover the deeper meaning of our own treasure of truth as we try to make it clear and convincing to others. The most potent means for the progress of the Church in the understanding and living of its own truth is the serious effort to teach it to the non-Christian world.

CHAPTER VI

"Sharing" and Beyond

THE CHRISTIAN WORLD MISSION IS MORE THAN A "SHARING OF OUR best," even a sharing of our experience of God. It is that, of course, and the use in recent years of the term "sharing" has helped to express the true attitude of the missionary. In the first place it means that the missionary, having found in Christ a supremely valuable experience of God, has not only a justifiable impulse to make that experience available to others but a sort of mandate from our common humanity to do so. This is very different from the dogmatic insistence that others shall accept our ways of thinking, our religious beliefs, and moral standards. The value of personal experience is one's own; to testify to it and to desire that others might also enjoy it is but the natural expression of human sympathy and kinship. It is hard to conceive that anyone should find something great and creative in religion without wishing that others might also have a similar experience. And there is no doubt that the strength of the Christian mission resides in those missionaries who have had such an experience.

It is not alone in religion that this impulse to share appears; in the scientific world there is a constant stream of reports and monographs making known the discoveries and reporting the studies which individuals have thought important. The same is true in every field of scholarship. Once I was asked by a professor of philosophy why we were interested in such a thing as missionary work. I told him that we felt it important to communicate to other people the main beliefs and convictions that we have as to the meaning of life. He couldn't see why we should want to do that; he said he had certain beliefs and convictions but that he had no desire to persuade others to accept them. That is the attitude of many cultured men and women about religion. And yet that teacher of philosophy was preparing to spend a sabbatical year studying a certain problem in the history of philosophy. Since that time he has completed the study and published the results. He discovered something of importance, and at once, and as a matter of course, shared it with the world—at least that part of the world interested in the study of philosophy.

A good many of these publications in science and philosophy, and in other fields of scholarship as well, have no immediate bearing upon the moral or even the cultural life of men. They are often so technical that few can understand them. Yet the scientists and philosophers and historians would feel greatly maligned if they were charged with merely amusing themselves by their research, or with merely making a reputation for themselves by publishing to the world the results of their work and the discoveries that they make. Scholarship is not utilitarian, but any serious scholar feels that the truth he is trying to discover, and in some degree does find, has real importance for human life, even though the common run of men who benefit by it may never be aware of the fact. That truth belongs to the race is the real premise of scientific thinking and it has prompted the complete openness and the fullest sharing among scientists. When the Curies finally perfected a method of isolating radium, and especially when it was found that radium had a therapeutic value in the treatment of cancer, they had before them the possibility of becoming rich by patenting the method. But in the true scientific spirit they scorned to do so; they shared without money and without price the price-less treasure they had discovered. Years of toil and actual pain had gone into the discovery, but once they had achieved it they renounced all property rights in it. After all, they did not make radium, they only discovered it. It was one of nature's gifts—but it was a gift to man, not to the Curies.

The Curies were right in their attitude. And the world at large applauded and approved their decision. Radium is a reality; it plays a certain part in human life, an enlarging part. That two people should labor and suffer and eventually die that mankind might become the beneficiary of all that radium can do, seems and is a noble thing. While at first the passion of the scientist in search of truth drove Madame Curie and later her husband to the discovery, there is no doubt that she derived the greatest satisfaction from the blessing radium brought to suffering humanity. The sense of our common humanity is deeper than the impulse to seek scientific truth. "Sharing" is more important than finding, because finding is personal both in the satisfaction it immediately gives and in the honor it may bring from others; but sharing satisfies our social nature and fulfils something in us deeper than the desire for individual well-being.

To share Christ and all that He means to our own life is the most natural and human impulse imaginable. No matter what other truths and values men may have found in other religions, here the Christian has a supreme treasure. It is not something that he has made but something that has been brought to him through a long tradition and at great cost, yet whose value he has discovered for himself. Christ is a reality; to the Christian He is the great reality. He has a part to play in human life of immeasurably greater importance even than that of radium.

There are some maladies of the human spirit that can never be successfully treated except by the potency of Christ's spirit. One feels moved to carry this analogy a bit further. Radium is everywhere in the world, but its pure force became available only by the patient labors of the Curies. The Spirit which is the potency in Christ is everywhere in the world and is indeed manifest in every great religion. But it was only through the long labors of the Hebrew prophetic line and finally in Christ that the force, as it were, was isolated and personified in pure form. The Christian Church has the keeping of the treasure. The healing of the sin which is man's most malignant disease can be accomplished by Christ; to be indifferent to the need of the world would be to deny the deepest impulse of human sympathy. In this instance it would prove that the Church did not really know the nature of the treasure it claims to have; further, it would prove that it did not even have the treasure any longer, that while it possessed the name and the form, the reality was lost.

There is another aspect to the idea of sharing which is thoroughly sound and Christian; that is the humility which it implies on the part of the missionary. The missionary commends not himself but the Christ to men. He comes as one who shares the common ills and needs of humankind to tell that he has found a way of essential salvation. It is a salvation which he himself feels he needs and of which he therefore assumes that other men will have a similar need. He is as much patient as physician, or rather he is a patient who has found the physician and who is eager to have others know that healing is possible. The fact that today we are more keenly aware than our fathers were—at least we think we are; I am not so sure—of the social aspects of the disease that afflicts us does not alter the case except to make the need of Christ even greater. The Christian Church is becoming aware that the solution to the great social evils of war and poverty and injustice is to be found *only* in the renewal of life and the change from selfishness to socialized personality which is the work of Christ. The very fact that Christendom itself has awakened to a realization of its own unfinished salvation makes very genuine the attitude of humility on the part of the missionary. "Sharing" becomes an invitation to all to receive the Christ personally and to experience the inner work of his spirit so that they may share in the common tasks to which Christ leads men. It is not that we ourselves have attained perfection or are made perfect but that we have found the way, the direction, and the true leader, and we want to enlist all men in the common enterprise. All this is implied in "sharing."

"Sharing" means also that the missionary takes a different attitude toward the non-Christian faiths and has a willingness to receive as well as to give. This attitude is not so exclusively modern as some think. There have always been missionaries with the most appreciative and open-minded attitude toward other religions. Fifty years ago, for example, Dr. George Newell went to Japan. After his retirement, I heard him speak as follows at the Annual Meeting of the American Board at Madison (October, 1930):

This matter of sharing the best that we have with the best that we find on the mission field is not particularly a modern idea, I think, at least not in my own case. I am not modern as far as age is concerned but it has been the principle upon which I have always worked. I was dumped immediately into a side street of a Buddhist community when I went to Japan (1887) and I found more Buddhist priests on every street of every city where I went than men or women of almost any other profession, so that I came early in contact with them. It was up to me immediately to find out what they were thinking, so I proceeded to the study of Buddhism. I found among my best friends in Japan many of the Buddhist priests. We used to share our thoughts and our experiences. How many of these Buddhist priests I have had in my home, how many I have visited in the temple, where we have shared hour and hour about, they reading the Buddhist book to me and explaining Buddhism and then I taking the hour for reading the Christian scriptures and explaining Christianity to them. I have had many teachers and have had many most interesting experiences. If there were time I should like to tell you about the half dozen or more of these Buddhist priests who found in the Christian scriptures a living vital spirit, a faith, which they could not find in their own scriptures and who are today preaching the gospel. Not all of them in the Kumiai church. One of them has long been a priest in the Episcopal church, preaching the gospel in Episcopal robes. I think of another with whom I worked two years and I received a letter from him beginning with the sentence, "Thanks be unto God for His noble gift." I introduced him to the Methodists and he has long been a preacher in the Methodist church. I can think of another who had a wonderful experience, something like the vision of Paul on the way to Damascus. He was at one time one of the greatest persecutors to our preaching in the city and yet he went through this wonderful experience. Through getting a Bible in his hands he began to study it for the sake of finding the weak points in it and he was struck with something which gave him a vision and which led him to Christ. He is today a preacher of the gospel, the editor of a paper called *Social Service*, and he is a fine outstanding man. There are others whom I could speak of; one was a Buddhist priest who was not only a priest in the temple but a teacher in the Buddhist schools and after something over two years he at last came out and said he could not stay where he was. He had seen a light, had found a way, had come in contact with a vitality through Jesus Christ that nothing of the Buddhist scriptures ever revealed to him. Just one word and I am through. He came one day and expressed surprise to find me reading the Buddhist scriptures and was more surprised to find that many of them had been translated into English. I would read some in the original and some in the English of a volume which contains most of the Buddhist scriptures that are used in Japan. I showed it to him and he asked if I would translate it back into the Japanese and in my poor way I started and translated sentence after sentence to the middle of the page. He asked me to go back and translate that once more, then brought his hand down on his knee and said: "I understand. I am ashamed to confess it, but that is the first time, I am ashamed to say, that I have understood what it means. I suppose I have read it hundreds of times, but I never understood it before." So you have the Christian missionary teaching Buddhism to the Buddhist priest.

But it cannot be denied that this is a new attitude for the Church generally. The Church is coming to see that a missionary, eager to profit by the culture and the religious teachings of the people to whom he takes the Christian gospel, is on a much better footing than the one who is moved by a blind prejudice toward all things connected with their religious faith. Such a missionary shows a personal respect for those with whom he works. This is a matter of very great importance; it signifies personal humility on the part of the missionary and lays the basis for true friendship between him and both Christian and non-Christian. It means that he is willing not alone to share with others what he has to give but also to have them share with him what they have. There is no unfaithfulness to his own religion in this mutual sharing. We may be perfectly certain upon the basis of commonly shared knowledge that

Judaism needs Christian truth to complete and correct it, but that does not mean that we cannot find in the Old Testament a perennial source of spiritual nourishment nor that we cannot look to fine personalities among the Jews for help and inspiration. Nothing is lost and much gained by the mutual sharing to which many missionaries are today sincerely committed.

A great deal of this sharing goes on as a matter of course. In every country I visited on a trip that took me around the world I found missionaries living on terms of personal friendliness and free exchange of thought with non-Christians. In Tokyo I met with a group of Shinto, Buddhist and Christian leaders who are accustomed to meet monthly. Many have read in *Re-Thinking Missions* of the similar fellowship in which Dr. C. Burnell Olds participates. In India I found the International Fellowship which is really an inter-religious fellowship. In Bangalore, Madras and Lahore I met with them. Hindus, Parsees, Jews, Moslems and Christians were present at the gatherings and they are accustomed to frank discussion of both their agreements and their differences. In Syria and Turkey I found missionaries who had intimate and respected friends among Moslems. "Sharing" in the finest sense of the word is a fact, and a fact to be rejoiced in. The truth of Christ—Christ Himself—is not anybody's private possession and will not suffer from open and friendly intercourse with men of every faith. "Sharing" is really based upon the faith of the affirmation in the Fourth Gospel: "I, if I be lifted up, will draw all men unto myself."

But the work of the missionary, as of every preacher and teacher of Christianity, goes far beyond any sharing of what he himself has or is. Our experience of God in Christ is never perfect or complete. What that experience is at any given time does not mark the limits of what Christ has for men. There would be a supreme conceit in our enterprise if it were only a matter of propagating our own acquired virtue and wisdom. It is because a certain type of dogmatism tends to make just that of the preaching of the gospel that men of humbler and broader minds have reacted against all religious propaganda. And if that is what anyone means by "sharing" then the term is only a modern expression of the old conceit of dogmatism. It signifies a limitation of the message to the understanding of the missioner and restricts the spiritual value to be transmitted to the actual quality of his life.

Certainly there must be in the life of the missionary something of that which he would communicate, some understanding of it, and some sincere embodiment of its meaning in his personality. But sincerity and reality in this respect do not mean that his own personality encompasses that treasure which he would give to the world. He is not merely sharing himself, but something far beyond anything he has yet attained, or indeed will ever fully attain. What he is really trying to do is to introduce men to a higher, to a divine and infinite source of that truth and grace in which he himself finds salvation. "For we preach not ourselves, but Christ Jesus as Lord, and ourselves as your servants for Jesus' sake. Seeing it is God that said, Light shall shine out of darkness, who shined in our hearts, to give the light of the knowledge of the glory of God in the face of Jesus Christ."[1] Those words of Paul state very clearly the true basis upon which the missionary and the preacher work. If the old dogmatism put the preacher in the position of trying to force the thinking of others into the forms of his own doctrine, there is at least a hint in the modern

[1] II Cor. 4:5, 6.

emphasis upon sharing that the missionary already has in himself something so valuable that everybody ought to have it. The focus is still upon what the missionary knows and is and has to communicate. But this only partially represents the truth of the matter; in effect it sadly distorts it. The true teacher is always trying to transcend his own knowledge in two ways; first, he is trying to bring the student face to face with the truth which he himself knows only imperfectly. Or, to put the matter more accurately, he tries to bring the one he is teaching into a direct experience of and interest in the reality with which truth has to do. He takes him into a laboratory if it is chemistry, or to the fields if it is botany, to the rocks if it is geology, etc. As a teacher he can indicate certain methods of study and pass on a certain amount of knowledge already achieved, but essentially his function is to confront the inquiring mind of the student with the real facts and objects that are to be known. He does not merely transmit to the mind of the student the system of ideas and explanations which he himself has already acquired.

The other way in which the teacher goes beyond his own mind and its contents is in his appeal to the mind of the student. Face to face with the facts the student becomes a learner in his own right. He profits by the ideas he gets from his teacher and by the suggestions as to method, but if he ever really becomes a chemist or a botanist or a geologist, he does it by first-hand and creative intercourse with the realities with which knowledge deals. Granted that most students do not go beyond their teachers and that they are content to think pretty much within the terms of the ideas they get from them; it still remains true that their knowledge becomes their own and acquires a much greater reality when they derive it from direct experience of the facts, than when it consists only in taking over the finished ideas of the teacher. Every good teacher rejoices in the student who goes beyond what he himself knows. The living mind of the student with its own capacities is as much a reality as are the objects with which knowledge deals. The true teacher seeks to awaken that mind and when he finds one that surpasses his own in its power to discover and understand he has his supreme satisfaction. But whether it be the ordinary man who does not make any new discoveries or the creative thinker who soars beyond all his teachers have ever known, the teacher does not merely give what he has; he brings a living mind to the experience of reality and the result is something beyond his power or desire to control. He does not merely share his experience or his knowledge; he puts the student in the way of having his own experience and gaining his own knowledge.

It is very much like this with the missionary. Paul said that the law was a "pedagogue" to bring us to Christ. The peda-gogue was the slave who led the boy to school; he was not even the teacher. So the missionary leads men to Christ, to the gospel and to the full content of Christian teaching. There is much more in that teaching and in the Christ than he himself has fully made his own, and there is an original activity in the mind of the one he teaches which will make its own discoveries and have its own appreciations. The missionary, therefore, is not merely sharing what he has; he is putting the other man in the way of having his own experience of Christ and making his discoveries of spiritual truth. Ordinarily those who are taught do not go beyond what they see in the teacher, but even so, his work succeeds in so far as they respond directly to

Christ and not just to the ideas and character of the one from whom they have learned.

But there are many who far surpass their teachers. With the person of Christ before them, with the thought of the Christian tradition to stir their minds, they not only see what others have seen but they get new insights and become creative teachers and leaders in Christian living. The finest fruit of Christian missions is this transcendence of the missionary in the lives of those who have learned through him. This is the source of the living Church in all parts of the world. The missionary does not really build that Church; it is created by the men and women who have made the Christian faith their own. The real leaders of that Church are those who learn not primarily from the missionary but from Christ.

So "sharing" as the communication of what we find of value, and as personal humility, is a true description of the Christian mission, but even in that sense it does not tell the full story. We must give more than we have and bring men to the experience of a Reality infinitely greater than ourselves. This goes beyond sharing, and were it not so, Christian missions would utterly lose their significance and become a grand expression of the spiritual conceit of men.

There is another word needed to characterize the Christian mission which may shock and startle. "Sharing" shows a certain amiability which pleases us and makes us feel that we have been delivered from the harshness of dogmatism. But if it means that we have lapsed into a loose and easy tolerance, then again we have misconstrued our responsibility. For there is a certain justifiable and necessary *intolerance* involved in the preaching of the Christian gospel, the intolerance of truth toward error.

What people ordinarily mean by tolerance is the willingness to let others say what they think and believe what they hold to be true. This is tolerance of persons, and the Christian, whether he be a missionary or not, ought to stand for it out of basic respect for the integrity of human personality. But tolerance of false ideas is a very different thing. To stand for the right of every man to speak his mind does not mean that no opposition should be offered when he says what we believe to be false and harmful. One cannot teach truth in religion, any more than in other fields, without opposing error. A large part of the teaching of Christianity anywhere is the combating and correcting of false ideas. So long as men believe that war is a normal and glorious thing there is a definite obstacle to the learning of the truth of Christ. So long as men believe that man's fate is fixed beyond any power of the man himself to change it, there is an error that obstructs the knowledge of truth.

The business of the Christian missionary is to indoctrinate men with Christian conceptions of God, of life, and of the true values of life. He has a positive truth to teach; it is a truth of ideas and principles and moral objectives. Wherever it is taught it must encounter whole masses of thought and systems that contradict it. It must be patiently taught so that it will be grasped by both mind and heart. Since one of the most important steps in acquiring the truth in any matter is the unlearning of false beliefs, the attack of the Christian teacher upon these false ideas must be persistent and relentless. He must no more tolerate false ideas of God and of human virtue than the teacher of science will allow his students to go on with wrong ideas of chemistry or botany. A teacher of mathematics will not tolerate the belief that two plus two is equal to four for one person at one time, and that it equals five for someone else at another time. Whatever his method of correcting the error he will insist that it must be abolished. Stern intolerance of inaccurate and false thinking is the foundation of true progress in knowledge anywhere. The open mind and free inquiry do not mean that men can trifle with truth or be permitted without challenge to believe and teach things that are in error.

It is the demand for openness of mind and freedom of inquiry that has caused us to make such a virtue of tolerance. And this has been historically justified. Intolerance has caused the Church too often to deny and suppress the free search for truth. That is still the official position of the Roman Catholic Church. So sure is the Catholic Church that it has the truth, and so fearful of the error that may oppose it, that it has taken a position of intolerance not only toward what it considers false ideas, but also toward those who hold them and toward freedom of thought and expression as well. This is one way to show concern for truth. But another way, and a sounder way, is to insist upon the freedom of every man to search for truth. And that is the way liberal Protestantism has taken. The results of this latter method more than justify it; in fact it is the only guarantee of the progressive discovery of truth. It is based upon a fundamental faith in the power of truth itself and also upon confidence in the essential honesty and capacity of the human mind. Of the latter, the Catholic Church is profoundly distrustful and it also shows lack of faith in the power of truth itself to win assent.

But while liberal Christianity stands squarely for freedom of thought and tolerance toward those who hold what we consider false beliefs, it is not less concerned than the Church of

Rome with truth and with the dissipation of error. Our whole mission rests upon the success with which we can get people to unlearn false religious beliefs and to acquire the substantial body of Christian teaching which constitutes the solid base and structure for Christian living. It is futile to assume that men who cherish pagan conceptions of themselves and God will ever really learn to live for Christian moral and social ideals.

There is also a certain *irresponsibility* in the enterprise of Christian missions. The missionary does have a sacred responsibility for the faithful teaching and living of the Christian gospel. This makes sufficient demands upon him. It makes it necessary for him to perfect himself so far as he can in the understanding of his message and of the full meaning of Christianity both in thought and life. It requires of him a mastery of the forms of thought and usually of the language of the people to whom he goes, and a competence in the techniques by which the meaning of Christianity is effectively made known to them. Individuals differ in all these things; some few become masters in them all; but those engaged in the work of missions realize that constant efforts must be made to enable the great majority to fulfill this responsibility.

But apart from that aspect of the matter and its admitted importance, there is a sense in which the missionary must learn to be irresponsible. Again it is the great missionary of the first century who gives us the true ideal: "I planted, Apollos watered; but God gave the increase. So then neither is he that planteth anything, neither he that watereth; but God that giveth the increase."[2] It is this kind of irresponsibility that the missionary must cultivate if he is to have courage and patience and

[2] I Cor. 3:6, 7.

power in his work. So profound is the change he seeks to bring about in the lives of men that he is likely to find himself in despair about ever accomplishing anything. Or, if he is of a confident and vigorous temperament, as the American is likely to be, and accustomed to manage things efficiently, he is at once confronted with the temptation to get whatever results he can in a limited period of time by the use of high pressure methods. Both these dangers are real; many have become discouraged by lack of visible response from those with whom they have labored, and there are too many who have gotten results, but of a superficial kind which have in the end become a scandal to the very name of Christianity.

The cure for both these evils is the realization that spiritual change cannot be managed and that spiritual growth is a plant that cannot be forced. The missionary above all men needs patience and faith to work for results which he may never see. He must feel responsible for planting and watering and cultivating as well as he can, but unless he can be content to leave the increase to God he is doomed to failure. This is true of all the effort of the Church to transform the life of men. There is no preacher who has not had to face the apparent futility of his preaching; there is no worker for social righteousness who has not been thrown back upon his faith in an undergirding force and purpose which can effect the results for which he labors. Man must labor, and leave the result to God. In a profound sense we are not responsible for the consequences of our best endeavors.

This kind of irresponsibility has been one of the finest parts of the missionary enterprise. Dr. Strong gives an excellent example of it in the early days of the mission in south Africa: "Reviewing his early labors Aldin Grout once said: 'I worked there as God gave me opportunity for ten years with various interruptions, and at the end of that time I could not point to a single convert or to a single one of my hearers of whom I could confidently say that he had been benefited by my message.' Then he added: 'It never entered my head to doubt that I and my fellow laborers were where God called us to labor.' "[3] Someone may say, "Yes, that was the natural attitude for one who held to the old absolute and dogmatic belief in the truth of the Christian religion." But there are two things to be observed as to that: first, men in those days were as subject to doubt and misgiving about basic doctrine and also their own vocation as they are today. Most church members of Grout's day probably thought of him, in so far as they knew of him at all, as an amiable fanatic or an impractical idealist. And the second is that the Church today, and not alone the missionary, needs as strong a faith both in the essential truth of its doctrine and in its call to make the gospel known to the world as that which moved Aldin Grout and his fellow-laborers. That is why I am insisting here and elsewhere that a strong conviction of the *truth* of Christianity is indispensable to an evangelical Church. The secondary results that give support and encouragement are often denied until any one generation has passed from the scene; our faith must span the generations and give us confidence in labors of which we shall never see the fruit.

There is an especial need today for such an attitude in the world task of Christianity. Many aspects of Christianity are being threatened. Radical changes in politics, economics, and intellectual culture have blocked some avenues of advance and may sweep away much of the structure of the Christian community in some countries. The powers of this world are becoming increasingly suspicious of a religion that is not amenable to

[3] William E. Strong, *The Story of the American Board*, p. 137.

nationalistic control and that interferes with the plans of imperialism. Even the mild degree to which the Church has in the
past and does in the present assert its Christian ideals interferes
with the ambitions of totalitarian states. And there is some
evidence that at least part of the Church is going to assert those
ideals more definitely and more vigorously than it has in the
past. The Church of Rome may betray its trust by sanctifying
fascism, which it partially justifies by its vociferous campaign
against communism, but the liberal Christian Church today is
pledged to stand for those very ideals of humanity, of justice,
and of freedom which the organized paganism of the day
scorns and seeks to destroy.

In such a state of world affairs the Church must have a
truth to proclaim in which it has such confidence that it can
afford to teach that truth, though for the present there is no
prospect that it can bear its normal fruit. There must be some
things in which we believe so strongly that we shall make
every effort to teach them to others no matter what the difficulties and the obstacles. Such teaching is the sowing of seed.
No one can be sure that the seed will germinate in the heart
of any individual. Even when it has germinated we cannot be
sure that external conditions will encourage or permit its
flowering in the full meaning of the Christian life. But we will
never sow the seed unless we firmly believe that it is good
seed, that it has the germ of life in it, that it is God's truth
and has power when received to create anew the spirits of men
and to generate the kind of community Jesus had in mind
when he announced the coming of the Kingdom of God.

Such a creative truth is the gospel of Christ. It is the supreme
responsibility of the Christian mission to preach it and teach
it and to encourage in every way possible the embodiment of
its meaning in life. But the vitality of that truth works within

the hearts of men by the mystery of God's own working, and too officious efforts to determine its movements may cause frustration and despair. If paganism blots out here and there the whole appearance of a Christian community, this truth may still live deep in men's hearts. Whether the harvest is to begin in a decade or a century is not the concern of the sower. We need a sort of cosmic confidence, an ability to give our all in an endeavor to make Christ known and to teach the way of His kingdom and then to leave the outcome to God with the serene confidence that He will bring into being that for which we now labor. This kind of irresponsibility is the only true attitude for the Christian Church and the Christian missionary.

The whole burden of this chapter has been the insistence that Christian missions is God's affair, that we, the Church and the missionary, are doing something at His behest. We are trying to impart more than we have, so it is not merely a matter of sharing even our best. We are committed to a Truth which is not our own subjective preference but a Truth as objective and as mandatory upon the soul of man as scientific truth is upon the mind; we must practice, therefore, a determined intolerance of all that contradicts that Truth, though we take great care that we violate no man's person and that we preserve the freedom of all to seek and speak the truth as they see it. That Truth is of God, and the vitality by which it works in men to recreate them and to build the Christian community is also of God; we therefore must teach and live faithfully, but not, presumptuously, assume responsibility for the results. "Sharing," therefore, as qualified by the intolerance of truth and the irresponsibility of faith, is the true method and principle of the Christian mission.

CHAPTER VII

The Two Poles of the Christian Movement

THE VITALITY OF CHRISTIANITY IN THE WORLD IS DUE TO THE FACT that it is not merely an organization or a propaganda but a *movement*. Subtending and pervading institutions and organized activities is a spirit which outruns them all and manifests itself in results beyond the devising and often beyond the expectation of the missionary. Were this not so the whole business would be abortive; the fact that it is so is due to the presence in Christianity of an original force which meets a deep and persistent need in human nature. The spread of Christianity is not an artificially induced activity but the vital outreach of a universal Spirit and the response to it of the spirit of man. Put more simply and more adequately, it is the activity of God using whatever men and methods the Church can furnish, and others, too, directed upon the religious need and nature of men. This being so, we ought to look upon the whole movement with a degree of reverence as for a spiritual activity in which we have a part but which has depths and outworkings that go beyond anything we ourselves plan. The most faithful performance of the things we can do ought to be coupled with a profound sense of our cooperation with something greater than we. Here is a joint working of the Spirit of God with the spirit of man out of which are destined to come results beyond our power to imagine.

In this spirit we may attempt an analysis of the Christian movement in our time and try to find a sense of direction which will guide our own plans and efforts. Conditions may change and are changing rapidly but there are some underlying factors that are not likely to change very much. They indicate two main poles of the movement—the Church, and the general influence of Christian thought and ideals in human society. In the grand scheme of things that develops in the New Testament the first stage is that represented by the figures which Jesus uses to indicate the minority role of the Christian fellowship.

Ye are the light of the world.

Ye are the salt of the earth.

They are not of the world, even as I am not of the world. I pray not that thou shouldst take them from the world, but that thou shouldst keep them from the evil one.

For narrow is the gate and straitened the way that leadeth unto life and few are they that find it.

This emphasis upon the fact that the real Christian fellowship is limited in number is true to the whole course of history and is fully borne out by the present religious scene. They are few, always, who make their own in any full sense the riches of the Christian faith and become creative participants in the Christian fellowship. Ideally they are the Church; actually the Church is largely made up of those who have been in some degree affected by Christian ideas and who in a general way believe in the Christian God. But there is always at the core of the Church those whose hearts and minds and wills are committed to the God revealed in Christ and who are struggling in terms of their own life situations to be Christian. When, therefore, we talk about the Church there is an embarrassing ambiguity that can never be entirely dispelled.

This is true, of course, in many other relations and we have

to make the best of it. A great deal of the effort to reunite the
Church or to do anything distinctly Christian regarding the
issues of social and national morality is tangled up in this
ambiguity. While officially, as it were, we must proceed upon
the assumption that the organized communions *are* the Church,
although disunited, and that that Church is opposed by the
world, as a matter of fact the greater part of those who belong
to the communions are by no means wholly committed to the
spirit of Christ which makes the Church of Christ one and
which condemns the greed and violence of the world. Rather
they *are* the world whose selfishness and materialism the ideal
Church opposes. And this is a defection that runs through the
Church from top to bottom. It is not alone the marginal member but the high ecclesiastic as well who is moved by the spirit
of the world. As in all human institutions the worst corruption both of mind and conduct has often been in the high
places. While today standards of personal morality are maintained pretty generally in the organized Church, the pagan
conceptions of human society which militate against a Christian world community find their support in the upper reaches
of the Church's life as well as on the lower levels. The tacit
assumption that a strong and united Church would deliver the
world from a paganism which has taken modern form in the
doctrine of the totalitarian state will not stand before the
testimony of history. Too often men have had to be delivered
from the Church itself in order to achieve liberty and to make
ethical and social advances. We would do well to fear any
official union of the non-Roman Church today; the plain fact is
that it is not yet truly the Church, and it does not yet live
sufficiently by the grace and truth and liberty that are in

Christ to be trusted with the power that organic unity would give.

Nevertheless, with this critical reservation in our minds we can accept as a reality the Church which is the salt of the earth and the light of the world and which is earnestly striving to be faithful to Christ and to live according to his spirit.

The last stage as envisioned by Paul and the Apocalypse and by Jesus himself embraces the world. The Church may be in opposition to the world but it is continually acting upon the world to change it. The whole cosmos is included in Paul's sweeping vision, "the creation itself also shall be delivered from the bondage of corruption into the liberty of the glory of the children of God." And the apocalyptist's prediction that "the kingdoms of this world shall become the kingdom of our Lord and of His Christ" is his dramatic way of reaffirming Jesus' promise: "Fear not, little flock, for it is the Father's good pleasure to give you the Kingdom" and his figures of the mustard seed and the leaven.

The Church which is consciously committed to the Christian faith and life, cannot, therefore, be indifferent to the world at large; an inclusive view of the operation of the Spirit of God in the world will disclose effects in the general life of society which change it in the direction of the Christian ideal. The world is not all bad; men outside the Christian Church and indeed outside all organized religious groups are still essentially of the same stuff as Christians are. They have spiritual aspirations, they have a moral consciousness, they have a need of God. Human nature and the questing Spirit of God are constantly meeting in unofficial but fruitful union God is busy with all humanity and not alone with those who have consciously entered into some religious fellowship and given themselves to the realization of the will of God according to some definite religious system. Were there not this universally diffused impact of God upon man and need of man for God the Church would dwindle and cease to be. But it is there and it constitutes the fruitful field for growth in the world of the Kingdom of God. The diffused but real influence of the teachings and ideals of Christianity constitutes, therefore, a most important part of the Christian movement. It must never be lost sight of, and so far as positive effort can be made the missionary has a responsibility to increase it.

When we look at the Church today in those parts of the world where Western missionaries are at work it does not seem to be a very impressive institution. It takes its place along with the school and the hospital as an agency for the communication of Christianity, but it cannot be said to constitute the most obviously important agency. It seems like leaning upon a broken reed if we put our main trust in the Church for the progress of Christianity.

These three institutions—the hospital, the school, and the Church—have been the main channels of Christian effort and they still are. There are sound reasons for the preeminence of this trinity of missionary service. Health, education, and region are vital interests of the individual man. Body, mind, and spirit are directly served by them. Any genuine concern for man as man requires that these basic services be rendered as well as may be; indeed, any large-scale transformation of society which does not eventually issue in health, education, and spiritual growth has failed to justify itself. A plan of economics, whatever else it might do, which ends by leaving men hungry; a theory or system of education that leaves individual men ignorant; a religious or ethical order that fails

to bring new life and grace to the individual soul; these mus
be counted as unrealistic, to say the least. The true test of the
Christian is always his downright interest in individual men
and his desire to bring to them whatever will make them
better and happier and more useful. This direct concern fo
men is firmly grounded upon Jesus' own manner of life. He
was the healer, the teacher, and the savior. No human need
was a matter of unconcern to Him; He left to others the
building of a theology and the elaboration of social techniques
and dealt directly and creatively with individuals. This was
His point of departure in the preparation of the world for the
coming of the Kingdom of God. It must always be the solid
base for the building of that Kingdom. And so, without any
particular planning of a grand strategy, Christian mission
have developed the hospital, the school, and the church a
basic forms of human service.

Of these three the hospital has a certain preeminence. Sick
ness and bodily injury are the most obvious of evils and men
universally desire to be delivered from them. The Christian
doctor with scientific medicine as his method can give relie
to many who without him would be condemned either to
lifelong suffering or to a speedy death. He can relieve pain
he can save life, he can help people in the most desperate
physical extremity. The moral and religious teacher anywhere
has to face inertia and unwillingness, even hostility, on the par
of those who need him. The doctor's patients receive him
gladly, and gratefully with amazing docility do what he tell
them even though it requires pain and self-denial. Because he
can give such service the doctor can most directly and per
suasively express the Christian impulse of love. Other Christian
workers often find themselves frustrated in their desire to do

good to men, but the doctor and the nurse can go to work at once and show their love for men by the most obvious kind of service.

Then, too, the number of those who come to the hospital and of those who are served through visits and clinics is very great. Millions of individuals have received this ministry of healing. It is true that in most cases the individual has a very superficial touch with a representative of Christianity; he may have the haziest idea or none at all as to why the missionary should come to his country and community and why the Christian people across the seas should build a hospital there, if indeed he knows at all that they have done it. They come and go without learning much about the teaching of Christ. Those who stay for longer periods learn something, but, generally speaking, we must set off against the great number who touch Christianity at this point the fact that they touch it very lightly and go their way with at best a gratitude to the doctor and the hospital for the particular service they have received. However, medicine furnishes the broad base in human service for the Christian mission, and despite the slight contact most patients have with Christianity through the hospital it has been in the modern period a missionary method of inestimable value. It has been that not as a direct evangelistic agency but as a supremely effective expression of the sympathy and concern for men which are of the essence of Christianity. That is a meaning that can be better conveyed by doing than by talking.

The school does not touch the lives of so many as does the hospital but it has a unique opportunity to influence those who come to it. Going to school involves a habit of years; they are the years of youth during which minds are developing and characters forming, and the school is directly occupied with the minds of students. Apart from the direct teaching of religion as a subject in the school curriculum, other subjects also are taught by Christian men and women and the school is administered by Christians. Spirit and attitude are better conveyed by the general manner of life than by direct teaching; this means that many, even, who leave mission schools without accepting the Christian faith are deeply affected by Christian ideals of life. There is no doubt that the most effective agency for actually communicating the thought and the spiritual and ethical meaning of Christianity in recent times has been the school. Wherever I went in the Orient I found that the strongest Christian leaders were those who had learned Christianity through years in mission middle schools and colleges. The astounding statement was made not long ago that there were more Christians in the National Government at Nanking—when Nanking was a capital—than in any other national government in the world with the exception of those of Great Britain and the United States. This is due to the fact that until recently about the only way to get a modern education in China was to go to a mission school and college. This marked influence of the school has not been due to compulsion; students in mission schools are not required to become Christians. In fact, in many schools the majority who graduate are not Christian, at least in formal profession. The tendency in recent years has been to make chapel voluntary and courses in religion elective. But the fact remains that those who go to Christian schools *learn what Christianity is* and even though they do not formally accept the Christian faith their outlook on life and their fundamental attitudes are deeply influenced by it.

Compared with the hospital and the school, the Church seems to be a rather negligible factor in the advancement of Christianity. The situation varies, of course, in different countries. The Church is relatively strong in Japan, weaker in India, and weaker still in China. This statement reports the impression of one traveler and does not claim to represent a factual or statistical study. If the impression is essentially wrong at any point it still remains true that it is the impression gained from some observation and much discussion with Christian leaders in the three countries named. I am speaking now of the relative strength of the Church compared with the hospital and the school. In Japan the Church is mostly urban, and has been from the beginning made up largely of the middle class, professional and business people constituting its lay leaders. While it is small in numbers it maintains a high standard of professional training for its ministers. In India the most striking single fact about the membership of the Church is the abnormally high percentage of former outcastes. This means that general standards of education and the economic status are low and that able leadership is often lacking. I asked an experienced missionary executive in India what was the chief problem of the Christian movement in India. He replied that it was the Church, that until the Indian Church was independent in leadership and financial support it could not be a real Church. He then went on to say that he saw no prospect in the near future of its becoming independent. This was said not as a criticism but as a statement of fact. It states plainly the basic problem that has to be faced by those who see the importance of the Church and who want it to become strong and self-reliant.

Still greater weakness is to be found in the Church in China.

In some ways the Chinese Church has a sounder base than the Church of Japan or of India. It is not, like the Japanese Church, restricted to the cities, but is dispersed through towns and villages. It has been estimated that there are seven thousand points in China where there are either churches or small groups of Christians. There was a time when cultured Chinese held aloof from Christianity, partly because of pride in their own superior culture and partly because most missionaries were not well enough educated to command their respect. But since China has turned at last from preoccupation with her own classics and has accepted Western learning, and since the Christian colleges and universities have made Christianity intellectually respectable, Chinese of all classes have openly favored Christianity and many have accepted it. The Church in China today, therefore, is both rural and urban and embraces all cultural classes.

There are large and ably led congregations in the cities, but the Church in China is made up for the most part of small groups who worship in quarters never designed for the use of a church and who are too poor to afford the luxury of a resident pastor. The problem of pastoral leadership represents a vicious circle. The great majority of the churches are not able to pay the salary of a college- and seminary-trained pastor. And the young man preparing for the ministry, seeing no opportunity for an adequately paid pastorate, or a congregation that would respond to a high type of preaching and teaching, does not take full college and seminary work. This means inadequate leadership for the churches. The fundamental problem is quite simple; it is the low economic level upon which the great mass of the people live.

I have put this case of the relative weakness of the Church

bluntly. In efficiency of organization, in professional standards of the leaders, and in the matter of equipment, the Church is quite obviously inferior to the hospital and the school.[1] This does not mean that there are not some strong congregations in all three countries, nor that there are not many individual Church leaders whose personal ability and whose professional training are of the highest. And the general situation is getting better due to well-devised programs of National Christian Councils and other agencies. We ought to recognize, also, that there are obvious reasons for the superior equipment and leadership of the school and hospital. They have been organized according to established standards and maintained by missionary money and government help until they could pay their own way, or partly do so, while the Church has taken people where they were and has had to create of them an organized body. No selective process based on age or competence for the special purpose (as in the school) has been possible or desirable; young and old, wise and simple, make up the Church. No highly trained staff (as in the hospital) can be maintained; for that matter the hospital takes people only when they are sick and gets rid of them as soon as it can, the sooner the better. But the Church must provide a life-long fellowship and service for all, and that means that the quality of that service so far as professional training and material equipment are concerned must ultimately be within the capacity of the people themselves to maintain.

It is against the background of this plain statement of the condition of the Church that I make the affirmation that the Church is the most important institution and agency for the progress of Christianity. There are perfectly good reasons for

[1] I would except Japan so far as my own observation goes.

this. The first is that the Church is the fellowship of Christian people and that Christianity as a living fact is embodied in the Church. This is not a particularly mystical fact, at least that is not what I mean here. Christianity is essentially a religion and the Church is the institution of religion. Membership in it is for life. People get out of a hospital as soon as they can, and even the school provides a spiritual environment for a short time only. But the Church provides a life relationship; the quality of that relationship in the end, therefore, is more important than the quality of service one gets in the hospital or the school.

There is also the tendency today for education and medicine to become secularized. They have their own professional standards and special objectives which can be served as well technically by those who have no religious interest as they can by earnest Christians. As in the home country most of these services are no longer looked upon as religious, so the tendency in the Orient is for education to stand on its own feet and for medicine to do the same. There are Christian hospitals in Japan, but nowhere are the people dependent solely upon them and some missions have no medical work at all. That is not now true of India and China but the drift is in that direction. We may hope that for a long time the Christian mission will maintain both schools and hospitals, but there is no doubt whatever of the tendency toward secularization of both. This would be so even apart from another factor that has now entered—that is, the positive efforts of governments to nationalize education. Mission schools everywhere are having to face this situation. It may mean a reasonable cooperation between governments and missions, as is now the case in varying degree in different countries. But, especially in war, or in case of a fascist trend it may mean the end of Christian schools. In any case it reveals the fact that government has a dominant interest in education and not only that it will eventually provide education for all but that in the meantime it claims the right to regulate what goes on in Christian schools. In a lesser degree a similar result may be expected in medicine; indeed, already the practice of medicine and the conduct of hospitals are increasingly subject to government control.

That leaves the Church as the one institution whose central interest is religious and which is professionally Christian. So long as it is permitted to exist it does so primarily and exclusively for religious and Christian ends. The weight of responsibility for the maintenance of the Christian religion and for its extension, and for the cultivation of the Christian life, rests squarely upon the Church. It is more important that it shall be a Church strong in the quality of its faith and life and in the vigor of its evangelism than it is that any particular educational or medical work shall be carried on. People generally see the value of education and health; they need no special Christian motivation to seek them. But the values of Christian faith and character are not so clearly recognized. They must be positively cultivated by and in a Church which is committed to them and which cherishes them. There is no other agency primarily concerned for them and pledged to their service. The Church is the distinctly and peculiarly *Christian* institution; Christianity is its supreme business and concern, its *raison d'être*. While other agencies may partially serve Christian ends, they also can be made subservient to other and quite different ends. The core of the Christian movement, therefore, is and always will be the Church itself. A wise missionary policy will recognize this. The theme for the meeting of the International Missionary Council in Madras next December shows that at this point the world Christian movement is on the right track.

But Christianity is never confined to the organized institution of the Church; it is a thought and a spirit and an energy; it enters into the life of men and works its changes in their mind and conduct by many means. In some ways the most impressive form of the Christian movement in the Orient to-day is to be found in the influence upon life in general of the teachings and ideals of Christianity. A few illustrations will be suggestive of this although in the nature of the case no accurate and adequate account of it can be given.

The modification of Buddhist practice in Japan under the influence of Christianity is now well known especially through the appearance of Young Men's Buddhist Associations and Sunday schools patterned in organization and program after their Christian prototypes. But there is also a widespread change of general attitude and an interest in social services which is new. One day I visited two large, well-equipped social centers in the city of Tokyo, both carried on in connection with Buddhist temples and operated by Buddhist priests. After being shown about by the priest detailed to act as host, I mentioned, in each case, the fact that it was very much like the work of many Christian social centers in my own country. Each time the priest said, in effect, "We are copying the Christian program; they did this first and we are following their example." There seemed to be no hesitancy in giving credit to Christians for setting the pattern; rather a sort of pride that they also conformed to it. Though it is out of harmony with the basic philosophy of Buddhism, present-day Buddhists in Japan are interpreting their religion in terms of social activity. It is quite patently a response to the lead and the stimulus of Christianity, and represents the best kind of influence of one religious system upon another.

Ethical standards and attitudes are also being modified by the impact of Christian thought and the best expressions of Christian living. A growing reaction against the practice of contracting girls to brothels in order to raise money under stress of desperate need has resulted in the passing of laws against this age-old custom in many of the prefectures of Japan, and in popular condemnation of it. The widespread inculcation of higher standards of integrity in the practical affairs of life by writers who have no connection with the Christian Church but who reflect Christian moral standards is observed by those who follow current Japanese literature closely. There is a good example of this in a recent play by one of the leading playwrights of Japan, Yamamoto Yuzo. The play is entitled *The Crown of Life* and is translated into English by Mr. Glenn W. Shaw. Its theme is the unswerving faithfulness to a business contract by a crab-canner on the coast of Hokkaido. This man encountered opposition by former associates which made it impossible for him to fulfill the terms of his contract. Rather than resort to the use of inferior crabs and other dishonest methods he endured the gradual loss of his business. In all this he had little sympathy and support from friends and relatives. The last scene shows him a dismal and defeated man, his business a failure and his house sold over his head for debt. But he has maintained his integrity. No moralizing has been done throughout the play and there has been no mention of Christianity, but the last scene closes with this postscript, which gives the play its name: "Be thou faithful unto death, and I will give thee a crown of life.—The Revelation of St. John the Divine, Chapter II, Verse 10." Mr. Shaw says that this represents a widespread inculcation of Christian ideals by poets, novelists, editorial writers, and others.

This kind of diffused Christian influence is even more apparent in India, and naturally so, since India has known Christian teaching longer than Japan and has been under the rule of nominally Christian Britain. At the close of the day's program of the International Fellowship in a bungalow twenty miles out of Madras I was given an hour to say whatever I would. I took the opportunity to ask the group, made up of Moslems, Jews, Parsees, Hindus, and Christians, what the Christian missionary could do in India that would be of the greatest good for India and that would be devoid of any real offense to the Indian people. Instead of answering my question they at once began to tell me what Christianity had already done for India. A Parsee woman said, "Christianity has profoundly affected the whole life and thought of India." Others spoke, one man denying that Christianity had done anything at all for India, but no one seemed to agree with him. Then Mr. S. S. Pillai, the chairman of the day, spoke. He is a Brahman and was then educational officer for the corporation of Madras. "Leaving aside the institutional aspects of Christianity," he said, "and its connections with imperialism, Christianity as it is seen in the New Testament teachings, in the life of Christ, and in the best missionaries, has been a searchlight thrown upon the vast, complex mass of Hinduism and has had the effect of distinguishing between that which is true and noble and that which is weak and base." Mr. Pillai is a devout Hindu and has no intention of becoming a Christian. Indeed, he went on to claim that

Christianity has brought no truth which Hinduism does not already have. Recognition of the pervasive and morally stimulating influence of Christianity by a devout Hindu, and one openly critical of some aspects and historic associations of organized Christianity, is most significant and by no means uncommon in India.

Mr. Pillai also drew attention to the chief asset of Christianity, the person of Christ. I think Stanley Jones was right when he said some years ago that Christ holds a preeminent place in the world and that there is no one else really bidding for the heart of the world today. Many in all religions are drawn to him and openly or tacitly recognize him as the most perfect revelation of the divine and the highest ideal of human character. The role of the great Person who embodies the meaning of life better than doctrines or institutions is no less today than it has been in the past; it is a permanent role in religion, and however inadequately the Christian Church has embodied His spirit and character, Christ still remains the source of life and grace for the world. Whether he can enter into the systems of the non-Christian religions and regenerate and reconstruct them until they become channels for his spirit is an open question; he is having enough difficulty with the Church and the religion that profess to represent him. But there is no doubt that the potency of his person and teaching is being felt throughout the societies in which the small Christian Church lives and that he is preparing the minds of men for a new day. In this all of his disciples rejoice. It is a sort of extra-curricular activity of the Spirit of God in which those elements by which Mr. Pillai defined Christianity, the teachings of the New Testament, the person of Christ, and the lives of his true followers, are used as unofficial but powerful means of changing the spiritual temper and the moral standards of the people.

So here are the two poles of the Christian movement, the Church, and the general influence of Christian ideas and ideals. Either one taken alone would be limited. The Church is, after all, small and insignificant in itself, and if it were all that constitutes Christianity not much would be heard of it. On the other hand, if it were only the general influence of Christian ideas the movement would soon become a vanishing thing. Ideas must have positive definition; they must be taught and propagated by those who believe them. This is the specific task of the Church. There is always a tendency subtly to change the meaning of ideas until their cogency and force are destroyed. A Chinese pastor told me that one of the important functions of the missionary is "to keep the doctrine pure." He did not mean technical theological doctrine but the essential meaning of Christian ideas as they are embodied in life. Non-Christian life and thought very easily absorb and then change those Christian conceptions. The fate of Buddhism in the land where it arose is sufficient warning of the way in which a religious system can be completely wiped out, not by frontal attack or outright rejection, but by this process of absorption and the final elimination of its central idea. But taken together the Church and the general influence of Christianity constitute a dynamic and creative movement in the countries of the Orient. It is of the greatest importance that the Church shall become strong and that it shall do its work of teaching and the cultivation of sincere Christian living in its own membership. And encouragement should also be given to the wider outreach of Christian conceptions of life with the full realization that that, too, is a medium for the activity of the Spirit of God.

These two poles of the Christian movement suggest also two types of missionary work that are needed. The first is the strengthening of the Church as such. Missionaries need more and more to be practical churchmen. It is no disparagement of the role of the teacher and the doctor to say that we need more emphasis upon direct service to the Church. This is not an easy thing. Nothing must be done to lessen the effort of the national churches to achieve independence both in leadership and in financial support. But the resources of the Church of the West and its long experience must somehow be put at the disposal of the newer churches of the East. Even financial help must be managed in such a way that it will not make for an attitude of dependence. Strong moral support and encouragement will be needed for churches small in numbers and surrounded by a non-Christian society if they are to grow and to maintain their vigor.

But there ought to be also a certain amount of Christian service which has no direct connection with converting people to Christianity or with building up the Church. This is needed for two reasons; first, Christian sympathy prompts us always to serve human needs. Christianity is not an international charity, as I have tried to show in a previous chapter, but it is never real unless it moves us to serve our fellow-men. Some degree of this service ought to go on and will go on for this reason. But there is another reason for it; it gives concrete and intelligible expression to the meaning of Christianity. It illumines the words of teacher and preacher. Christianity is neither a philosophical speculation, nor an academic ethics; it is a life and a life of active sympathy and human helpfulness. This is recognized quite generally in the Orient where Christianity is known as the religion of activity. Sometimes that term is used in negative criticism implying that Christians lack spiritual depth. More often it is the admission of a reality and power in Christianity that religion ought to have. Whatever form of service we can render, therefore, ought to be made a part of the missionary program or should remain so. Specialists in agriculture, in social service, in health work, in community organization, whoever can do anything that will enrich and improve the lot of men, are needed as missionaries. They should first of all have a real faith and a clear knowledge of the meaning of Christianity; they ought to live their own lives openly and sincerely as Christian believers; but they need not try to convert except as the layman in normal intercourse may make his testimony. They need have no direct responsibility for the building of the Church; they can leave that to others; but they will represent the Christian movement as the embodiment of its impulse to serve men on the level of their basic human needs.

Part III

Objectives of Christianity

CHAPTER VIII

Christian Truth

WE HAVE BEEN DISCUSSING THE WORK OF CHRISTIANITY IN THE world, and some of the principles of its progress. Now we shall try to make clear, in terms of the modern mind, what its main objectives are. We are accustomed to the expression of those objectives in such words as these: "the evangelization of the world," "winning the world for Christ," "making the world Christian," "bringing all men to a knowledge of God in Christ." A more modern form of expression might be "the extension of the Kingdom of God into the whole world."

I have no desire to discredit these phrases; they disclose very well in the conventional language of religion the evangelical character of Christianity, and certainly in religion we should be free to use without apology the language of religion. But it is always useful to examine our religious objectives from the perspective of the present mental outlook and rephrase them so that they will gain a new cogency. That is what I hope to do in the present chapter and in the two that follow it. No one would dare attempt to forecast all that is in the divine purpose for man or all that would come out of a well-done task of Christian teaching and living in the world, but the kind of ends envisaged in the Christian enterprise are not hidden; and the more clearly we see them the better we shall do our part in that enterprise. I venture to define the goals of Christianity in history, therefore, as (1) Christian Truth, (2) Christian Personality, and (3) Christian

Community. These goals will constitute the subjects for our thought during the remainder of the book.

It is because Christianity claims to be true that it is of necessity a missionary religion. For truth, unlike custom and culture, is universal. That is one reason why religious systems must contend with each other in so far as they take themselves seriously. The great missionary religions, Buddhism, Islam, and Christianity, are religions which do take themselves seriously both in the moral and the intellectual sense, and claim to have a truth which is universal. Islam claims to get that truth by direct and miraculous revelation; Buddhism claims a truth discovered through profound meditation first by Gautama and since then by all who faithfully follow his method. But in both cases it is the truth about man as man and his ultimate place in the total scheme of Reality. Truth in religion is never merely speculative or academic; it is the secure basis of living by which man may attain to salvation. It has its moral ends, but also its intellectual form, and both must be grasped if religion is to do its full work. The technical form that truth takes in religion is theology. It may seem to the layman and even to many ministers that theology is abstract and remote from practical interests, even those of the religious life. But that is a misunderstanding of the true nature of theology.

Our present-day technical civilization should help us to see the importance of theology because it too involves much abstract intellectual effort. Engineering is the key to much of our practical life today. The engineer is the man who knows how to do things, to build bridges, to bore tunnels, to construct factories and power plants. He has skill, but back of his skill lies intelligence. Industry is depending more and more today upon the research in chemistry and physics upon which the industrial engineer depends. A new material appears; we all use it in our steering wheels and eat off it at the lunch counter. It becomes commonplace. But it has come into being because research workers, using the most highly developed theories of molecular construction and the operation of chemical forces, have labored in their laboratories. Mathematical formulae which deal with purely conceptual terms have entered into the mental processes by which eventually a plain black substance can be put at our disposal to do a better job for us than wood from a tree or metal from a mine.

We do not all have to master this highly specialized knowledge to get the benefits of it. Nor do we all have to become theologians in order to have the values of religion. But we ought to realize that such a process is involved in religion and lies back of its practical values, and that someone has to devote himself to it. There is nothing essentially mysterious about the process and there are no privileged persons or classes who have exclusive rights to this kind of knowledge. Every minister of religion should be, although many of them are not, a competent theologian. The intelligent layman should have a clear understanding of the main doctrines of his religion, just as everyone who drives an automobile ought to know the function of the ignition system and of the carburetor, and be able to change a tire. The average one of us is not an Isaac Newton, but we can and do understand the law of gravitation which he discovered. Some say that one day the ordinary educated man will understand fairly well the theory of relativity. None of us could write plays like those of Shakespeare, but we can all enjoy them. In fact, often the highest achievements of the intellectual and the artistic genius are precisely those which are simplest and most universal in their appeal to men.

I write these things to try to dispel the feeling that the matter of truth in religion is beyond all but theologians and that it doesn't matter much anyway. Truth, when once found, is likely to be simple and quite intelligible; and it is a necessity for successful action in any realm. Our conduct is always an expression of our conceptions of life; if we profess beliefs contrary to it, that simply means that we have not examined and understood our own thoughts. In religion, at least as much as in anything else, life grows out of our real beliefs. There is no other point at which honesty and clarity of thought are more needed. "Can two walk together except they be agreed?" asked Amos. A very pertinent question. If the two are not agreed as to where they are going one will go one way and the other another way. On the other hand, if they both voluntarily go to the same place it is proof that they have the same idea even though they may express it in different words. A religion is an agreement as to where we are all going. The Christian agreement is Christian truth. It differs from the Buddhist agreement and the Moslem agreement and the communist agreement and the fascist agreement. It is exceedingly important always that we shall know to what we are agreeing. The clear understanding and teaching of truth, therefore, is one goal to which an evangelical Christianity must give itself.

But now we cannot sidestep two questions and since they are closely related I shall put them both together and then see if we can get a satisfactory answer to them. They are (1) What is truth? and (2) Why "Christian" truth? Recently I received a letter from a highly competent Christian teacher in Syria raising this last question. He put it something like this: If we are sincerely seeking for truth is it not a tacit prejudging of the case to talk about "Christian" truth? The Moslem in like manner is looking for "Moslem" truth and also prejudges the outcome. Why should we not say frankly that we are looking for truth and keep an open mind; is not this the way we find truth? And will not a Christian or a Moslem prejudice effectually prevent its discovery? One cannot but admire the intellectual honesty of this man, and wish that there were more like him in the world, both in his honesty and in his perspicacity. A right answer must be found to his question or the whole Christian mission is on an insecure foundation in an enlightened world.

But before we can attempt such an answer we must pay some attention to the first question, What is truth? As a matter of fact, like "love" and many other words, it has different meanings, even in our common speech. When we say that "seven times eight equals fifty-six" is a true statement, we mean something different from what we do when we say that it is true that "Charles Lindbergh made a continuous flight from New York to Paris." In the first case we mean that the statement is logically consistent; this is the character of all mathematical truth. It is not necessary for us to have seven of anything—as, for example, marbles—and then add seven more and still another seven until we have eight sevens and so can count up and find fifty-six. We are not talking about marbles or anything else; we are talking about the logical relation of numbers. But in the second case we are making an affirmation about a particular man and a specific act that he performed and our statement is true only if it corresponds to what that man actually did.

What is truth? In the first instance, it is logical consistency but may not have to do with anything that exists. It is equally true that minus seven times minus eight equals minus fifty-six. In the second instance, it is correct correspondence between our statement—and our thought, of course—and the specific facts to which it refers. We think in these ways all the time and truth means first one and then the other thing, sometimes both. There are other meanings for truth, for example, that of the pragmatist who says that that which works is true; that is, if I think something and then act upon my thought and my action is successful, then what I thought was true. We also often use the term "truth" in that sense. The first of these three meanings of truth deals with the logical relations of ideas, the second with the relation of ideas to facts, and the third with the relation of ideas to future actions.

But there is another meaning of truth which is vital for religion. That is a truth that has to do with the nature of Reality. "Reality" is a general term including the nature of God and of man and of the purpose and meaning of life. First of all we have to live and we must live in this universe. Truth about ourselves and the ends of our existence is all-important and that involves truth about the Being or Reality with which our destiny is bound up. The most important question must be raised first; humanity cannot wait until the learning of centuries has made an adequate answer possible. It must answer that question the best it can at the start. So religious faith precedes in time both science and philosophy and always precedes them in importance, for it is religious truth that answers this question. We may all agree that we should do the will of God, but what is the will of God? We may all agree that we should be good, but what is goodness?

We may all agree that we should strive for the ideal, but what is the ideal? We might agree that we ought to love God, although not all religions teach that, but of what character is the God whom we should love? Now, the truths that will answer these questions are not merely true in the sense of being logically consistent, nor do they merely refer to specific facts, nor are they merely beliefs that work. All these meanings of truth must be taken into account but we must go beyond them and find a meaning that fits this case. Such is religious truth.

There is a difference between scientific truth and religious truth; not that they imply the use of different faculties or organs of knowledge. The same mind is employed in both and in large measure it acts in the same way. But there are significant differences. Perhaps the fundamental one is that science is morally neutral, or irresponsible, as to the ends for which the knowledge it gains is used. As has often been pointed out of late, science discovers the way to make antiseptics and other things that lessen pain and save life; but it also concocts poison gas and high explosives capable of inflicting great pain and destroying life. Scientific truth is involved in both kinds of products. It deals exclusively with natural facts and forces. But religion is supremely concerned with ends and purposes and so religious truth is a truth about moral values. What men do with themselves and their possessions is the essential concern of religion, and the truth it claims to have is a truth about what men ought to do. Let us leave it at that, then, and not bother about other differences; science ignores the *ought* in its exclusive absorption with what *is* and especially, in this day of applied science, with

what will work effectively, while religion is radically interested in the *ought*.

There is also a difference, although a lesser one, between
philosophical truth and religious truth. The general task of
philosophy is to describe in terms of the most general and
universal ideas the nature of "process and reality," that is, of
the whole of things. Now, one branch of philosophy is ethics
and ethics does deal directly with conduct, with both ends
and means. In this it operates in the same area as does religion. Moreover, philosophy speculates about the nature of
God, or the Absolute or Ultimate Reality. What, then, is the
difference between philosophy and religion? The first principle of philosophy, as a reflective exercise of the intellect,
is impersonal, impartial, dispassionate thought. Of course,
few philosophers ever conform fully to this principle, for they
also are men with fears and hopes, with loves and hates.
But, as philosopher one must serve faithfully the abstract
idea, for that is philosophical truth. Now, religion embraces
just those elements of our mental life that philosophy holds
at arm's length, namely, love and hope, devotion, self-com-
mitment, whole-hearted action; that is, it has to do with the
whole man. Not caution but the constant acceptance of the
decision of life-and-death is the nature of vital religion.
Religion does not stop with the rational concept of God as
the Absolute or as the Supreme Good; even before formulating any rational idea it commits heart and will to the service
of God. The religious man is primarily a devotee, a lover; the
philosopher is primarily a critical thinker. It is hardly necessary to point out that the former is more fundamentally and
completely human. Religion and philosophy are in closest
interaction among all advanced peoples and indeed they can-

not well get along without each other. Sometimes religion cools down into a philosophy, as in the Deism of the eighteenth century and the Vedanta philosophy of India, with the consequent playing down of will and feeling. On the other hand philosophy tends to become a religion, since all men must live, and we have neo-platonism and Comte's Religion of Man.

The truth with which religion deals heads up in the idea of God. What God does and will do follows from what He is. The true relation of man to God depends upon the divine character, and the essential nature of morality depends upon the will of God for man. Manifestly no natural science can tell us anything about God, for God is not a natural fact or set of facts to be observed, measured, and used for man's purposes. Philosophy can help; it can construct a concept of God, although never one that is free from rational difficulties, and it can by rational criticism expose crudities in our thought of God. But it can never point men to a real God, who, not as an idea commanding the intellect but as a Person commanding heart and will, makes the religious life possible. The God of religion is not merely thought of but responded to—as real, indeed, as the great Reality; He is the ultimate ground of life and hope and love.

Each religion has its idea of God and of His dealings with men. When, therefore, we say that Christianity is true we claim that its idea of God is true. That does not mean that it will differ wholly from the idea of God held by other religions; there are some points at which all the advanced religions are in substantial agreement. For example, Islam, Judaism, and Christianity all agree that God is One. They would also agree that God is Good and that He wills that man should be righteous. They would further agree, and many other religions would join them in this, that God will pass judgment upon men according to their moral conduct. But more or less wide divergence will appear when we examine the meanings of goodness and even of oneness. And when we get at the basis of the divine judgment upon human life we will find very serious disagreement, which means that the quality of character encouraged by the different religions will vary and that the sense of security with which man lives his life will be based upon different principles.

In the light of this, let us return to the question, "Why Christian truth?" It is, of course, because upon these ultimate matters of God and the spiritual basis of life in man's relation to Him, Christianity has its own distinctive affirmations which are at the heart of the whole life of worship, of moral endeavor, and the courage and joy that faith brings. This truth of Christianity has grown out of the experience of the race and the long reflection upon the spiritual life as it narrowed down to the specific advances achieved by the poets and prophets of Israel. Out of that process of thinking and living and the interaction of life and thought upon each other in both personal and social aspects of human experience emerged the noble conception of God as One, as Holy, as Merciful and finally as Loving. Amos, Micah, Jeremiah, Hosea, Isaiah, all these and many more, most of them unknown, added their insight and their spiritual daring to the development of this truth through lives lived in conscious response to the God about whom their thought was becoming ever clearer and more adequate. Then came Jesus of Nazareth, who made his own both their thought and their experience of God. His knowledge of God was simple and immediate like our knowledge of a rose; like our knowledge of one whose will becomes our own will and with whom we love in the same manner and with the same quality of passion. Undoubtedly the God that Jesus called "Father" completely possessed his whole personality and determined the quality of his feeling and of his conduct and character. His knowledge was living. He was not merely representing God or telling the truth about Him; he was revealing Him.

We really come here to a still different meaning for truth, that is the truth that is embodied or actualized, made concrete, which, in regard to man, means personal. This is what an illustration always is. The only true illustration of what we mean by airplane is a real airplane. If one is shown to us we still need much explanation of the motive power, the principles by which it operates, the science of aviation, etc., and we need to take a ride in it to know how that feels. We could go further and learn how to pilot one, then how to repair, and even to make one. There is no end of things that we might learn about the airplane, and always new things; but to have that actual airplane before us which embodies all the meanings that we might be called upon to learn and which is a reality with many relations and possibilities which we may never learn, furnishes us with a concrete experience of airplanes of a different kind from all that we could get in thought and imagination by being told about it.

What God is as a Being-in-relation-to-man is thus illustrated by the person of Christ. All that Object of faith which any man can in some way experience in his own thought and feeling becomes concretely real in Christ. There is much correction of our impressions to be gained when such an illustration of divinity is given to us, and new meanings appear, but it is essentially a correction and completion of our own vital knowledge of God. To the end of our days we shall be occupied in more perfectly understanding what we see and in more fully embodying in our life the possibilities and the meanings of the God we have come to know with such concreteness in Christ. In one way, therefore, the truth of God that we have in Christ is final or ultimate; that is, the reality of God is disclosed in him. In another way, however, we shall always be learning the meanings for life of that revelation. So it is with all things. The reality of the human body has always been an object of our experience; nothing could take the place of the concrete fact. But the sciences of physiology and anatomy and other more special branches of knowledge having to do with the body are bound to advance. Incomplete or false ideas have never meant that the body did not exist or was not what it was. They have simply meant that men's thought about it has not been right.

"Truth," therefore, as we use it in religion is an equivalent for "Reality." "Truth is one," we say. "We seek a direct experience of Truth," "the mind was made for Truth," etc. What we actually mean is Reality. What we seek in religion as in life generally is not some idea or combination of ideas but fact and reality; in religion that means God. Because we have given this meaning to Truth with a capital "T" we can say of Jesus that he is the Truth. He was so completely one with God in thought and will and love that the reality of God as Personality is known when we know Christ. We have heard about the airplane and all it will do; but what we want is to see and use an airplane; no amount of knowledge piled upon knowledge will make up for the fact that no one will show us an airplane. We cannot ride from New York to San

Francisco in even the most perfect idea of an airplane. It comes to the same thing in religion. "Show us the Father and it sufficeth us," said Philip. It is not an unreasonable demand upon anyone who would speak for God to man. Since it is a truth of character, of spirit, of personality, that religion professes to impart, it is not only reasonable to ask that the supreme religious teacher shall have the right ideas and words, but also that he shall *be* in his spirit and character and personality the reality to which ideas and words refer. That is the crucial test of the ultimate validity of the revealer of God. If it is not possible, then some unbridgable chasm forever yawns between God and man and probably religion is not true at all. If it is possible then we should not only be willing to be convinced that it has happened but we should be morally certain that it has happened or will occur. That it did occur in the person of Jesus Christ is the basic faith of Christianity. "The law was given through Moses; grace and truth came through Jesus Christ."[1]

When, therefore, Jesus said, "He that hath seen me hath seen the Father," He showed full awareness and accepted full responsibility for the character of the true religious teacher. Any religion must in the end stand or fall by the answer it gives to man's quest for truth about God in terms of a person who teaches and embodies that truth. Unfortunately the whole matter of the nature and of the self-disclosure of God has been so bound up with miraculous and mythological conceptions that in order to make the affirmation that Christ is the true revelation of God, Christian thought has had to resort to ideas of a virgin birth, an immaculate conception (without which the virgin birth is not effective), and a

[1] I John 1:17.

strange dual-nature doctrine of the person of Christ. But the simple religious truth is there, none the less, and if it is not there mankind has not yet been given a convincing revelation of God. It is the conviction of the Christian that he finds God in Christ; all meanings of truth converge upon the reality that is there disclosed; Truth merges with Reality.

This is "Christian truth." It does not mean that there is not much truth both in ideas and in life to be found in all religions. It is not only Jesus Christ in whom the reality of God is found; in some degree He is to be discovered and is revealed in every "true" man, for man is made in the image of God. But no other has exhibited the qualitative completeness of God's love and goodness and moral wisdom as does Jesus. I say "qualitative completeness" advisedly, for the difference between the full revelation of spiritual reality and the partial is not quantitative—so much more or so much less —but a difference in quality, somewhat like the difference between the master artist and the one who is almost a master. The two are not different orders of being; the master is not a miracle; nevertheless one is and the other is not that which all recognize to be the goal and ideal of all artists.

For a Christian to present to the world the Christian truth which centers and is realized in Christ is not a matching of idea against idea so much as it is the offering of an historical illustration of what all the ideas are trying with greater or less success to represent. It is a sort of matter-of-fact thing. So long as no one has seen an airplane the argument may go on as to what one is like, or, perhaps, whether there is any such thing. But when all are brought to the airplane and given freedom to examine it, test it, and ride in it, the question of its reality is settled and all have the same basis for answering any particular question about it. Not all are equally competent, even then, to answer questions, for we must learn how to know an airplane even when one is presented to us. But we have the actual object before us and in so far as we can qualify we can learn from it. I know that this is a very crude and inadequate analogy, even misleading if pressed too far, as are most analogies of spiritual matters. But the main point, I think, is evident: that Christ is a fact, a real person; that he is what the Christian means by God so far as God has a human and moral meaning and is of significance for living and for the lift of hope and confidence in the promise of life. The Christian can say, "I have heard with the hearing of the ear, but now mine eye seeth." It is not a report but a reality that we present to the world as the Truth, Christian truth.

This historic revelation of God in the person of Jesus Christ did not end the discovery of God by individual men but initiated a new era in which every man is enabled to have his own direct experience of God. This is what is meant by the Holy Spirit. Jesus showed a remarkable combination of positive authority and reliance upon the free response of men. What he did say he said with an assumption of complete confidence, but there were many things that he did not say. Regarding those things he placed no limits of method or conclusions upon his disciples but left them freely to find the truth. "When he, the spirit of truth, is come he will lead you into all truth." That is the charter of complete spiritual and intellectual freedom which lies at the very roots of Christianity. But the spirit of truth is the Spirit of God and the Spirit of God is God as directly experienced. What Jesus was saying was that continual progress in spiritual truth is to come by the continual experience of the reality of God. What he did, himself, was to give humanity a clue, as it were, as to how one might recognize God and as to the right attitude of mind and spirit for those who would find Him. His own character is the clue. The finding of God has become for the Christian a much more human and moral and simple thing than one might expect. It has its terrible aspects, especially when His Spirit convicts us of sin and when we contemplate the prospect of life apart from Him. It lays stern demands upon us even to complete self-denial and self-sacrifice; "if any man would be my disciple, let him take up his cross daily and follow me." But it gives to the Christian a sense of being at home in the universe, a courage and a joy that cannot be destroyed by any of the defeats and disappointments of life.

Under the influence of Jesus' life and teaching and the continuing experience of God which they have made possible there have developed systematic statements of truth in the form of ideas which constitute Christian doctrine. Many elements have entered into this development, and success has been far from complete. The first thing Christian thinkers had to do was to take the current intellectual forms largely shaped by Greek philosophy and try to express the meaning of Christian experience of God in those terms. Had they refused to do so they would have shirked a primary responsibility, for a teaching that claims to be true must seek expression in the forms of thought of the common mind. That is one form of universality. The mind that experiences God and the mind that constructs general ideas is one and the same mind; the content of the Christian experience, therefore, was bound to seek expression in the most adequate conceptual forms. This was something of a hazard that Christianity had to accept. The intellectual life has its own peculiar faults and vices. For one thing, thinkers have allowed their professional interest in the intellectual life so to dominate them as to falsify the experience. This was the curse of scholasticism, which suppressed both scientific and religious progress. Its essence was the *a priori* method, the insistence upon deductive reasoning from certain premises and assumptions. This opposed the free inductive study of nature in science and the free development of religious thought upon the basis of personal religious experience.

But with all this artificial restraint upon the expression of Christian truth in the form of ideas or doctrine, and in spite of divergences of doctrine when freedom was asserted, there still remain certain large-scale affirmations of truth that can be made almost universally by the Christian Church, and there are substantial agreements in idea which lie back of differences and which are hidden only by the insistence of each communion upon the precise terminology in which it has traditionally expressed those truths. However, we need not expect complete agreement in the realm of ideas, and more important, we should not expect that ideas, however great our agreement, will ever perfectly or adequately express the reality of God and His impact upon the spirit of man. Not even in natural science, not even in physics, the most exact of the sciences, do ideas tell the full truth. They seem sometimes to interpose a veil between the mind and the reality. At best they half reveal and half conceal its nature. Man must *live* in the physical world to gain the most immediate knowledge of it. So man must live in God to know Him. Christianity assumes the responsibility and liberal Christianity always claims the freedom to explore all the possibilities of thought and to express as well as may be the truth which it has in the person of Christ and in the experience of God which he has made possible, in terms of ideas and systematic doctrine. This is a realm of freedom and progress. There is no finality in this quest; the finality is found in the ultimate reality in which religious experience originates, just as there is finality in the facts of nature with which science deals.

The free search for truth in religion which my friend in Syria most wisely insists upon is of the essence of the Christian method despite the fact that the Church, both Catholic and Protestant, has distrusted it and often suppressed it. What does it mean? For one thing, it means freedom to find and publish the facts about the history of religion. This has meant in Christianity the facts about its own historic existence. Those facts are not all pleasant to know; the Church of Rome still suppresses them wherever it can, and one of the useful accomplishments (of a negative kind) that the Protestant Reformation achieved was to bring them to light. But the facts of Protestant history as well are sometimes humiliating for a Christian, especially the cordial support of the Church to political states, to imperialism, and to economic exploitation. Within liberal Protestantism there emerged in quite recent times an objective, competent and rigorously honest scholarship which has told the Church the truth about itself in a way that has dismayed part of the Church but which has given a new sense of self-respect to another part and made it more conscious of the true nature and responsibility of the Christian faith.

Another set of scholars, with equal technical ability and with similar courage, have examined the literature of the Bible and given a true account of its origin and development.

Theologians, with free minds, have undertaken the interpretation of Christian truth in the light of the best modern thought and have disposed of some of the dogmas which have cramped the spirit of the Church and obscured some of the meaning of its message.

This is liberalism in religion, in Christianity—the freedom to go to the facts in all the historic expressions of religion and the freedom of the Christian to commune with God directly and to root his religious life in that experience and then to think honestly about it and speak freely of it to others. In all the penitence of penitent liberals today let us be sure that we do not surrender or renounce this essence of liberalism. If we do, we turn our backs on Jesus of Nazareth and do despite to the Spirit of Truth which he promised as the continuing presence and availability of God for his disciples.

In regard to the relations of Christianity with other religions we seek complete freedom and honesty in the study of origins, scriptures, and history. It would be a wholesome thing for Moslems to subject the Koran and the development of their doctrine and the course of their history to a scholarly treatment as competent and as objective as that which has served so well the cause of truth in Christianity. It is that for which such men as Sir Mohammed Iqbal plead. In fact, Moslem scholars have already begun the making of a critical text of the Koran. A great deal of research has been done on the literature and history of Oriental religions. A vast amount of mythology is cleared away or revealed to be mythology by such studies, but the essential characters of the religions are brought to light and the real values they have for human life are made more available.

Eventually the central idea and revelation of God in each

religion is disclosed. Moslem truth and Buddhist truth and Hindu truth confront Christian truth. No one will be found completely untrue, but there will be differences regarding the ultimate nature of God and of His purpose for man. There will be found a significant difference in spirit, in character, and in the representation of God's dealings with man. In this the Christian asks nothing better than that the world shall look upon Christ as he is and hear his words as the New Testament records them. We must then reverently leave each man alone with him. There is a sort of high rivalry between Christ and Gautama and between Christ and Mohammed. Each man must choose for himself which he will follow, each must decide which one speaks most truly of God, which has the answer to the deepest question of the soul. It is difficult to get an unclouded comparison. We all have deep prejudices and there are so many other things that interpose between us and the original revealers of God—racial and social and political ties and habits of private life. But the persistent seeker after God can penetrate these barriers, and the devotee of truth in religion will eventually face the claims of Christ.

In conclusion let us refer once more to the meanings of truth already defined and see their application to religion. In so far as truth has to do with the correspondence of ideas with fact, it calls for an objective and unrestricted investigation. Religion as history is the field of this search; no suppression or distortion of the historic fact should be tolerated. Liberal Christianity has stood resolutely for this kind of truth regarding its own religious tradition; now, with good conscience, it seeks the same truth in all questions of fact regarding the non-Christian faiths. Likewise, it opposes all arbitrary denial of rational criticism of religious doctrines. Special pleading, begging the question, and clouding the issues by appeals to prejudice are as immoral in religion as in any other realm. We must realize, however, that the process of rational criticism and construction does not lead with absolute certainty to truth. It is sometimes more effective in revealing error than in establishing truth; and it also may end in paradox, as, for example, the paradox in philosophy of the one and the many or of identity and change; in science, of continuity and discontinuity; and, in religion, of divine sovereignty and human freedom. But honest thinkers are always ready to admit the extremity of rational thought when they arrive at such a paradox; they will not try to hide the paradox on their own side by rhetorical affirmation, nor to make unfair polemical capital of the paradox of an opponent's position.

In the meaning of truth as an intuition of Reality which at the behest of life leaps beyond fact and reason and answers the question of the ultimate meaning of life and the nature of God, each religion has its answer more or less clearly given. Christianity gives its answer in the conceptions of the Judeo-Christian traditions as purified, reordered, and personified in Jesus Christ. Truth as concrete Reality is found in his person; it is not so much to be argued about as it is to be presented for each man to make his own response freely. The pragmatic meaning of truth, after many centuries, also has its force. Its testimony is not always clear. Christian truth is always caught and sometimes submerged in a complex of many other influences which determine the course of human thought and character. But, as I have tried to show in the first chapters of this book, the normal fruits of Christianity are an enhancement of life and an exaltation of human character which are of evident value. It is these fruits of Christian truth in human life that an enlightened evangelical Christianity today consciously seeks. The two remaining chapters will attempt an exposition of Christian personality and Christian community which are the two main consequences in human life of the vital progress of Christian truth.

CHAPTER IX

Christian Personality

CHRISTIANITY IS HEIR TO TWO MAIN LINES OF DEVELOPMENT IN its sense of the reality and value of personality. One is religious and the other is rational; both are strongly ethical. The religious source is the ethical monotheism of Israel, and the rational or philosophical source is Greek. The prophetism of Israel and the rationalism of Greece thus lie back of the conception of personality which is concretely embodied in Christianity from the beginning. The center of personality in Hebrew religious thought is the moral will; it is because man is a being who can obey or disobey the commands of God that he has both importance and responsibility. Apparently man alone of all creation can by his own volition either obey or disobey his Creator. The whole significance of life centers in this fact; it is the foundation of Hebrew religion. It gives man his spiritual place, and a very high one, in the universe. "What is man, that thou are mindful of him? . . . Thou hast made him but little lower than God and crownest him with glory and honor."[1]

The sense of value of the individual person is not found at first even in the Hebrew religion, however, but emerged only slowly out of a prior condition in which not the individual but the clan or tribe or nation was the moral unit. It was due to a specific moral development in Israel that this predominance of the social unit in man's relation to God, which they shared with the rest of the race, was modified by

[1] Ps. 8:4, 5.

a realization of the direct moral responsibility of the individual to God. Personal morality appeared as an innovation. It was not originally the Israelite with whom Jehovah made His covenant, but Israel. The "social gospel" in this respect was the primitive form of Hebrew religion. When one encounters in the modern Orient the dominant sense of clan or caste and the relative submergence of the individual in the family one is face to face with the original and natural form of the moral consciousness. It was out of this and as a departure from it that a certain type of vigorous moral individualism arose in Israel. In the Greek world a similar thing occurred; there ethical earnestness expressed itself in terms of rational definition and systematization of moral virtue. In general the Jew was interested in will and the Greek in intellect. The one held conscience subject to the command of God, the other to the idea of the Good. One was a religion culminating in the will of a good God, the other was a philosophy culminating in the rational authority of idea of the Good. Israel found the sense of cosmic order in the unity of a single divine will; Greece found it in the rational nature of Being.

The combination, opposition, and interaction upon each other of these two points of view, each deeply rooted in the reality of human experience, explain much of the development of Christian thought. There is in each one of them the seed of individualism. Will and reason alike are functions of personality. The individual who is willing to accept the danger and the responsibility can act upon his own moral decision and think his own thoughts. But let it be understood that this goes against the course of nature and tradition. The natural thing is for the individual will to assert without criticism the will of the tribe as embodied in its habits and buttressed by its mythology, and to reflect the social tradition as to beliefs and sentiments. Society still has a profound distrust of the individual who claims this moral and intellectual freedom, and visits various penalties upon him. Sometimes those who believe themselves to be defenders of individual liberty today are the most intolerant of all who, in the exercise of liberty, question the present habits of society and propose new ways. They are really defenders of a cultural collectivism, which, parading under the specious banner of individualism, opposes as dangerous the free exercise, even in the most moral and rational manner, of individual judgment. Such judgment is in fact both dangerous and revolutionary. But it is social solidarity and not individualism that speaks in those "individualists" who oppose it.

Our purpose here is not to discuss the philosophical aspect of the development of the idea of personality, but only to point out that there is the intellectual as well as the moral basis for it. When men turn away from custom and the mythologies that support it and use the tool of rational thought they have entered a realm of universal principles and ideas. It is only an individual mind that can do that and so take the open road to truth and freedom and progress. Christianity has benefited by the great tradition of Greek thought although it has often sadly mishandled and misunderstood it. Modern individualism is usually, and rightly, traced back to Descartes (d. 1650) so far as its intellectual roots are concerned. Descartes' platform was the complete competency of the individual mind to know truth. As a good Catholic he professed submission to the Church in regard to spiritual matters, although he actually invaded that realm at more than one point. But, despite his personal recognition of the authority of the Church in matters of religion, once he had asserted the competence of the individual mind to know truth, the cat was out of the bag, and others with equal zeal for truth but less piety soon claimed the full liberty of thought which is the basis of modern individualism.

But it was in the moral realm that the Hebrew found the key to personal worth. That moral conscience was so strong and so sure that it became the basis for criticism and revision of religious ideas. One of the most amazing episodes recorded in the Old Testament is the meeting of Abraham with Jehovah at the oaks of Mamre.[2] Abraham, reasoning with Jehovah to persuade him not to destroy Sodom if any good men were to be found therein, argues thus, "That be far from thee to do after this manner, to slay the righteous with the wicked, that so the righteous should be as the wicked; that be far from thee: *shall not the Judge of all the earth do right?*" What a presumptuous thing it was for a man to undertake to instruct his God in matters of morality! But it was a typical expression of the conviction that righteousness is supreme, and that the metaphysical status of God himself (that is, his mere power) is not to be held superior to the moral law. A mere man, with right on his side, may dare to make demands of divinity. *Right* is Lord and no *Power* dare disregard it. Of such was the stuff of the moral consciousness in prophetic Israel. The obvious logic of it is that the supreme God is Himself the supremely holy and righteous One. And this logic is fully expressed in the main prophetic tradition. Men speaking for Jehovah stood before kings and condemned them for their wickedness, as Nathan denounced David. They assailed unjust judges, the powerful aristocracy, and even the

[2] Gen. 18.

priests. They even pronounced doom upon temples and sacred shrines because the rulers and the people were not faithful to the moral commandments of Jehovah. What a magnificent manifestation of the freedom and the moral integrity of the individual conscience! The moral person sits in judgment upon the authorities, the traditions, the social prestige, and the religious life of the people, and in the name of God demands reform and righteousness of conduct.

Two influences operated to make this sense of personal responsibility and moral dignity not the prerogative of the prophet alone but a general quality of the moral life for all. Both issue from the destruction of the national state at the time of the Exile. With Jerusalem no longer the religious capital where, on behalf of the whole people, the priests might worship Jehovah in the temple, the doctrine of individual moral responsibility was developed. Jeremiah[3] and Ezekiel[4] reject specifically the idea of clan responsibility which was expressed in the proverb, "The fathers have eaten sour grapes and the children's teeth are set on edge." Jeremiah declares that "everyone shall die for his own iniquity: every man that eateth the sour grapes, his teeth shall be set on edge"; and Ezekiel expounds the same idea, summed up in this fashion, "The soul that sinneth, it shall die: the son shall not bear the iniquity of the father, neither shall the father bear the iniquity of the son; the righteousness of the righteous shall be upon him, and the wickedness of the wicked shall be upon him." Thus the individual person became the moral unit in man's responsible relation to God.

The other influence, closely connected with this shift from

[3] Jer. 31.
[4] Ezek. 18.

the nation to the individual in the moral life, was the insistence that righteousness should be a matter of the inner spirit and that the law of righteousness was to be found within the heart. So in a noble passage in Jeremiah we find this charter for the essential freedom and competence of the moral personality: "But this is the covenant that I will make with the house of Israel after those days, saith Jehovah: I will put my law in their inward parts, and in their heart will I write it; and I will be their God and they shall be my people. And they shall teach no more every man his neighbor, and every man his brother, saying, Know Jehovah; for they shall all know me, from the least of them unto the greatest of them, saith Jehovah: for I will forgive their iniquity, and their sin will I remember no more."[5]

Out of the original dominance of group custom and tradition which has been universal in the race Hebrew moral consciousness gradually made this discovery of the individual conscience and so of a constitutive element of moral personality. The dignity of man is found in the integrity of his moral will. The basic relation of man to God is a relation of moral responsibility. The individual is not merely a member of a human social group but each and every man has a direct relation of moral competence and responsibility to God. The supreme law of his life is not the mandate of his clan or tribe or nation and its interest, but the will of God. Nor is that God the God of Israel alone, but, as Amos and Isaiah already insist, He is the God of all tribes and nations; the moral will of God is the cosmic law. Here Hebrew religious consciousness meets Greek rational thought in the assertion of a uni-

[5] Jer. 31:33, 34.

versal authority for the individual mind, moral and rational, which designates the person as a free, responsible, and creative being. Individual persons claiming and nobly exercising these prerogatives strengthened and dramatized the doctrine. These were the prophets, the saints, and the martyrs.

The meaning of personality finds its truest embodiment in Jesus of Nazareth, and its most explicit application in his teachings. He affirmed and developed the idea of inward goodness and made purity of motive and sincerity of the essence of righteousness. The Sermon on the Mount is largely given to this teaching. It was man as man, not man as a Jew or a Samaritan or a Greek or a Roman, that he defined in the duties which he imposed and in the privileges that he guaranteed to those who followed him. And here the circle is complete; this insistence upon the elemental nature of human personality in its immediate relation to God is Christian individualism; by the same token it is Christian universalism. A man is a man for a' that. The full scope of brotherhood, or of fellowship, is the race. Since the human race is not organically one in social and political organization, there is no visible fact to represent this universalism. This seems to be a denial of universalism; and it is. Strangely enough the assertion of that universalism must be made and actually is made by the moral individualist who refuses to be dominated by the claims of class or national loyalty and, because he is a man, claims the fellowship of all men. The only way he can give full expression and honor to personality in himself is to claim a universal bond with all persons.

This is so plain and so basic in the teaching of Jesus and all authentic Christian doctrine that it would seem almost gratuitous to repeat it today. But the logic of the natural social morality of the class and the clan and the nation has asserted itself with such passionate force today that this Christian doctrine needs to be taught and interpreted with greater earnestness than ever. No kind of internationalism, not even the world mission of the Church, can long survive unless the universalism based on Christian individuality is taken much more seriously than it has been of late. The Christian world and the Christian Church itself have limited fellowship to national groups and to exclusive communions, and so furnish visible facts that deny the oneness of the race and even the unity of the Church, and interpose class prejudice between a man and his God. The true character of personality is not seen until it is clearly recognized that group characteristics of any kind are secondary, not essential. That means that the elementary right of criticism of all limited group conduct is inherent in the nature of personality. This is not said in any academic spirit nor without recognition that practical life makes it psychologically impossible, or practically so, for the mass of men to think much above or beyond their own class limitations. The affirmation of a universal humanity for all of us requires an act of "faith" and a religious passion that will prompt us to undertake enterprises for its realization that contradict much of the temper and practical organization of our human life. Those who work for peace today, or for economic justice, or for the Christian evangelization of the world are working against the current of practical organization and natural social morality. But they are acting true to the Christian conception of personality and they seek the universalism which it implies.

The dignity which moral freedom gives comes from the fact that God has made man free; in this there is both glory and shame. Freedom is the prerogative of a mature being and man is morally a child. The course of history or of any individual life reveals the waywardness and sinfulness of man in his use of freedom, and not alone sin due to evil intent but mistake and moral perversion due to ignorance and sheer incompetence to administer aright the powers of a free person. On the other hand, the triumph of good men over all the things that oppose and entice the moral personality is an impressive testimony to the fact that man is made in the image of God and that he is capable of great achievements. It is hard to maintain any doctrine of his total depravity in the face of the facts, just as it is impossible to hope for his moral salvation by his own unaided efforts. Religious thought has a tendency to go to extremes, and to claim either that man is wholly bad and completely lost in sin with no moral competence whatever, or else to make grand claims of his intrinsic nobility and in effect to deify him. Judeo-Christianity does not admit either extreme, but treats man as a being with real moral capacity but with constant need of divine help because of his moral and intellectual limitations. That may seem a rather unexciting estimate to those who like absolutes, but it is true both to the facts of common experience and to the clear teaching of Jesus and his first followers. Man is relatively free and relatively able to live a good life. His freedom is relative to his own powers and all the conditions of life which circumscribe his conduct and even invade his mind to influence what he wants to do. The range of freedom can be enlarged by constant moral effort and a severely critical judgment upon one's motives and it can be almost completely lost by failure to make such effort. But neither ability to act nor knowledge of how to act in the interest of goodness is ever absolute. The Oxford Groupers may well take their four absolutes as ideal goals, but when anyone claims to have fully attained them he is simply self-deluded.

When, therefore, we speak of the absolute value which Christianity gives to human personality we do not affirm either the actual or the possible moral goodness of man upon the basis of his independent being or action. It is because of his relation to God; put simply, it is because God loves man that man acquires and has sacredness and value. A real absolute enters into his life and becomes at once a basis for hope of infinite personal attainment and a source of restlessness and tension in this relative life that he must live. God has a purpose for him larger than he can comprehend and yet of which, in times of spiritual aspiration, he feels the imperious attraction. The uneasy consciousness of his freedom and the infinite possibilities that beckon him fill him with discontent. Too often he seeks to fulfill the longing for larger things with gross and egoistic satisfactions, and there ensue tragedy and failure and sin. Since it is because God cares for him that he has his personal value, so it is only as he also learns to love that he can realize that value in actual conduct and character. The full meaning of personality as Christianity conceives it cannot be understood apart from the quality of the divine Personality. Christianity accepts and reaffirms the moral freedom and responsibility which it inherits from Judaism and Greek thought, but it completes the idea of personality by making love central and regulative. God is a Holy Will and man is a relatively free will whose duty it is to obey God. But more fundamental still in Christian teaching, *God is love.* It is because God is perfect love that he is perfect Personality; it is because man also can love that he is true personality; and it is because God loves man that man is a being of infinite worth and has a destiny of infinite achievement and joy. The over-emphasis of Barthians upon the sovereign will of God and of the necessity of man's unquestioning obedience to Him tends to throw us back to a pre-Christian Hebrew prophetism and to obscure the true Christian conception of both man and God, that is of Personality itself.

The moral relationship as conceived in Christianity is a relationship between persons, either between human persons or between man and God. There is no abstract moral *law* which is more basic than personal will when the will is moved by love. God is free, because He loves perfectly, and love is of the essence of freedom. More basic than freedom of the will in moral life is the freedom of love. The will prescribes a law, or a command to be obeyed; love makes its bid for the heart and seeks to win a free response of love. Human freedom is thus derived from the fact that God is love and love can accept only a free response. In the actual exigencies of the moral life we all need to hold ourselves responsible to formulated rules and moral principles. But Christian righteousness goes deeper and seeks the free response of the heart to the God who loves, and who asks for love in return. Jesus and Paul and John insist upon this. Jesus summed up the whole law in the two commandments which are one, to love God and our neighbor.[6] Paul, apart from his great hymn to love in First Corinthians, explicitly rests the ethics of Christianity upon love as prior to all moral law: "Owe no man anything save to love one another: for he that loveth his neighbor hath fulfilled the law. For this, Thou shalt not

[6] Matt. 22:34-40.

commit adultery, Thou shalt not kill, Thou shalt not steal, Thou shalt not covet, and if there be any other commandment, it is summed up in this word, namely, Thou shalt love thy neighbor as thyself. Love worketh no ill to his neighbor: love therefore is the fulfilment of the law."[7] And the first epistle of John, in a treatment of love which in some ways reaches greater depths and higher heights than does Paul in I Corinthians 13, makes love for one's neighbor the essence of morality and even declares knowledge of God possible only through love: "Beloved, let us love one another, for love is of God; and every one that loveth is begotten of God and knoweth God. He that loveth not knoweth not God; for God is love."[8] These quotations from the New Testament are not exceptional; they represent the general agreement of both gospels and epistles. It is true, as some are insisting today, that Christianity requires obedience to the will of God. However, even as regards that, the insistence of Jesus was not so much on the *will* of God which all agreed in his day is supreme, but upon practical *doing* of God's will, upon the translation of religious recognition of the divine will into ethical expression of it in the normal relations of human life. This is always Jesus' strong emphasis; the Barthian today has shifted it back to the purely religious point at which it had run to seed in Jesus' day. But, even so, Jesus and Paul and John go beyond obedience to love and consistently differentiate between customary Jewish religion and morality by making love and not "will worship" or mere obedience the true touchstone of man's relation both to God and to his fellows.

It is even insisted that love for man practically expressed in

[7] Rom. 13:8-10.
[8] I John 4:7, 8.

ministry to his needs is proof of the reality of the kind of love that God wants. Such is the lesson of the parable of the Good Samaritan. In the picture of the final judgment in Matthew 25 those who are approved are those who were not consciously serving God but who did love and minister to men; it came as a surprise to them that they had been doing His will. In the first Epistle of John the same point of view prevails and is expressed in an explicit contrast: "If a man say, I love God, and hateth his brother, he is a liar; for he that loveth not his brother whom he hath seen, cannot love God whom he hath not seen."[9] This represents well what may be called the Christian humanism of the New Testament. What Jesus did was to put his finger upon the noblest element in man's nature, his sympathy and his impulse to love, and elevate it to the status of a supreme ethical impulse. In this capacity for love he finds the true nature of personality and the basis for moral relations; further, it is the point at which man is one with God in nature and in creative power and impulse. It is the key to our knowledge of God. When we say that God is a Person what we mean most of all is that He loves; when we say that man is a person, we mean that he has the capacity for love and for relations with other persons and with God upon that basis. Both the theology and the ethics of Christianity rest back upon this conception of personality and upon the character of man's relation to God and to his fellows which follows from it.

So persons are more important than abstract moral laws and the true moral relation is one of free persons who love one another. That is what Paul meant when he said that we are not under law but under grace. A law cannot forgive, but a

[9] I John 4:20.

Person can. A principle operates impersonally; but a Person formulates principles and changes them to effect the essential personal good that he wills to do to persons. Christian morality and Christian religion begin in the freedom of personality to create and to desire good for other persons and it ends in the free fellowship of persons who have realized and who use their capacity for love. There are intermediate or lower stages of righteousness and religion in which men obey moral laws and submit their wills to the commands of God, but the whole intent of Christianity is to disclose the full character of personality both in God and in man in the freedom of the spirit which love realizes. This is a conception of life that is hard for men to maintain. The rule of rational principle or of moral commands seems more natural and stronger. Paul encountered the tendency among Christians to revert to the Jewish law. His epistle to the Galatians is a powerful protest against this and an exposition of the freedom of the Spirit. "For freedom did Christ set us free," he declares; "stand fast, therefore, and be not entangled again in a yoke of bondage."[10] But Christians all down through history have either not been able to comprehend the meaning of their freedom or have feared to exercise it. The sovereignty of God has seemed a greater and stronger thing than His love.

The meaning that Christianity has given to personality emerges from this brief survey of the teaching of the New Testament and from our glance at the Jewish and Greek heritage of Christianity. From the Greek came the lesson in the intellectual power and competency of the mind by which an individual can free himself from bondage to accepted beliefs and superstition and know truth directly. From the Jewish

[10] Gal. 5:1.

tradition came the sense of personal moral integrity, which first set itself against the prevailing idea of God and which later caused prophets to speak in the name of God against all unrighteousness. Jesus and his first interpreters went deeper and did for the heart what the Greeks had done for the intellect and the Jews for the will; that is, He freed it and declared its impulse of love to be divine. This, of course, is not the selfish desire or the passion which seeks to possess either persons or things for private and exclusive enjoyment. The love that constitutes the heart of personality and whose freedom is of the essence of Christian righteousness is the infinitely outgoing impulse of creative good will. It is the secret of God's creation and of His redemption of men. Why did God create man? Because it is of the nature of love to create and to bestow itself freely. But love cannot bestow itself completely except upon a being that can receive it and love in return. So God must create man and then educate him and finally win him to a communion of love. Christ embodied that meaning. He loved and gave himself and sought in return the love of men. But no one can receive his love who will not himself live by the same love. It is not finally a matter of obeying commands but of loving. To be a true and free person one must release the impulse of love in his own heart which is the real likeness to God in him.

The result that Jesus sought is this full achievement of free moral personality. He states it explicitly in the Sermon on the Mount although the idea is consistently set forth in all his teaching: "Ye have heard that it was said, Thou shalt love thy neighbor and hate thine enemy: but I say unto you, Love your enemies and pray for them that persecute you; that ye may be sons of your Father who is in heaven: for he maketh his sun to rise on the evil and the good, and sendeth rain on the just and the unjust. . . . Ye therefore shall be perfect, as your heavenly Father is perfect."[11] Men who are like God in this deepest spring of their being are the fruit that Christ and Christianity seek in the world. Here is a true account of the nature of personality. In order to understand it we have had to survey the slowly developed insights of Greek and Hebrew and finally the bold revelation which Jesus made of the essential freedom of the heart. Reason, will, and heart are the abiding elements of personality and the greatest of these is the heart. We have found it necessary to turn from man to God to find the full meaning of personality because human persons are defective in all its qualities. The greatest Greek thinker did not claim that Truth was circumscribed by the thinking of his own mind; he held his mind responsible to the Idea. The Hebrew prophet did not claim that his own will was good but spoke in the name of the Holy God. And Jesus held before men nothing less than the infinite love of God as the true expression of personality in its deepest power and character. The reason why we can say that Jesus revealed God is that his love was pure and perfect. He specifically disclaimed knowledge of some things,[12] and even refused to be called "good," for, he said, there is none good but God.[13] But he did reveal God perfectly in love, a love which gave freely and which included even his enemies. This, too, is the revelation of man, for man is destined also to be a person, living freely and creatively by love. In this God and man are one, only in God love and therefore personality are fully real-

[11] Matt. 5:43-48.
[12] Mark 13:32.
[13] Mark 10:18.

ized; in man they are but potentialities. The purpose of Christ and the mission of Christianity is to bring to birth and full development the latent personality in which love is the motive power and the essential nature. Paul declares that this is the cosmic purpose: "For the creation was subjected to vanity, not of its own will, but by reason of him who subjected it, in hope that the creation itself also shall be delivered from the bondage of corruption into the liberty of the glory of the children of God."[14]

There is no break, therefore, in Christianity between religion and ethics, at least as to basic motivation. Religion involves theology and theology must use its own terms and work out a consistent set of ideas to explain religion. And ethics must develop principles and define methods and general objectives, for Christian men live in a finite world and must constantly translate their motive of love into specific forms of conduct. But the theology is explanatory and the ethics is instrumental; the root of the matter in religion is love of God and in ethics is love of man. And love is the supreme function of personality. Christian religion and Christian morality are rightly understood as the free relation of persons seeking to realize their own nature as love. God is a Person and men are persons; the basic relation of man with God and of man with man is personal; this is what is meant by saying that Christianity is theistic; it is also what is meant by saying that Christianity is ethical. The only really moral relation is a relation between free moral persons. Christianity seeks such a relation between God and man and between man and man. There is no assumption of equality with God in this: God is the Creator, the Father, and men are His creatures, or better, His sons.

[14] Rom. 8:20, 21.

God is the true and perfect Person; men are far from perfection although that is their goal. All human life is pointed toward God as Ideal, as supreme object of desire, as the one Reality. But while there is not equality, there is genuine likeness and identity of nature. The gulf between man and God is a moral abyss, not a radical difference of nature. Were it not for the fact that a sameness subtends that gulf then there could be no relations between God and man, but the relation of love is always possible and God is constantly pressing upon the human spirit for a free response and for the creation of a vital communion.

Once man responds to God's love that love becomes the ethical motivation in human conduct and seeks a bond of fellowship with other human persons which extends into human life the same relation that man has with God. This is the actual process of the growth of personality in us men, or, to use religious terms, this is growth in grace.

The essential freedom of personality is the key to the understanding of familiar Christian and biblical terminology. Dr. Hendrik Kraemer[15] uses the term "religious realism" to characterize the language and the thought of the Bible. What he means, I think, is the basic assumption in the Bible of the personality of God and of the direct personal relations between God and men. That is, persons are real and the nature of men's dealings with God is personal. The "grace" of God which Paul sets over against the Mosaic law assumes, with many, an unnecessary character of mystery and even of miracle. Because of His grace God forgives sinful men. He bestows His grace upon the Christian and enables him to conquer sin and live

[15] Hendrik Kraemer, *The Christian Message in a Non-Christian World* (Harper & Brothers).

the life of the Kingdom of God. How can God do this? The reason why it seems so great a mystery is that we think of God as a law giver and a judge, not as a Person. There is no grace in law or forgiveness in justice. But a Person can show grace and can forgive because a Person is a free being capable of loving, indeed whose essence it is to love. There is, it is true, a mystery in all this but it is the mystery of life and love and not of the act of grace. Knowing God as the Christian does, it would be unintelligible and infinitely dismaying if He did not forgive and bestow His grace upon all who can receive it.

It is the goal of Christianity to mediate this grace to the world and to develop persons who will live by it. This is God's purpose in Christ and it is the historic work of the Christian Church. Because every man is a being with the capacity to develop into a free personality the service of men is a first charge upon Christian love. Christian service does not seek a reward but it does seek a result and the result is personality. Nor is it some separate "soul" within the actual man which is to be saved. If I may use a special term to indicate the actual man that we see before us in his full reality as body and mind and spirit, I shall call him an "empirical personality." It is this real being with which Christian love is concerned. He has quite elementary needs—food, health, self-respect, opportunity for work, friendship; and he has deeper needs for spiritual satisfaction and supreme need for God. Now, Christian love does not abstract from this empirical personality certain "religious" or "spiritual" elements which it will serve. The man, so treated, is not a reality. Perhaps some day, in another sphere of existence he may be just a soul or a spirit. But now he is a man, an empirical personality, and the authentic Christian impulse is to serve him as he is. Some would ignore the spiritual service the man needs and unwittingly debase him thereby, and some would scorn the physical and social aspect of his life as not of spiritual moment, and thereby sacrifice reality to a specious spirituality. But Christianity really binds men together with a sincere concern for all that affects the life and well-being of one another. Whether it is health or hunger, knowledge or worship, employment or political liberty—all these affect the empirical man, though some point off to other realms and some are of limited importance. But it is the man himself who is important in the eyes of God and so of the Christian. Christianity seeks thus a full-orbed love for man and a mutual service which will give complete reality to that love in the lesser things while it seeks for each man the full richness of communion with God and the fellowship of the saints. The conditions of human life and the forms of service and cooperative effort for Christian ends will change, but this basic goal will remain the same.

In this present world Christianity should enter into the struggle for personality with a clear conviction of what it is doing. In the central shrine of spiritual consciousness it seeks to make men aware of themselves as sons of God. It should strive also to establish in their ways of thinking the essential Christian pattern of personal-moral relations as basic. Christianity has its own "ideology," although the term has a foreign accent. Transcending mechanistic ideas or merely naturalistic conceptions of man, and denying the political ideology that makes man an instrument merely of national glory, Christianity stands for the intrinsic worth and essential freedom of man. This idea of personality encounters as deeply rooted misconceptions in the great religions as it does in secular systems. In Islam it is the arbitrary and absolute sovereignty of God. In Hinduism it is the mechanical operation of Karma and the impersonal idea of God that lies ever in the background. In Buddhism it is the defective sense of the reality of personality both in God and in man. Religion and morality alike suffer from the deficient or defective conceptions of personality found in all these faiths. It is the mission of Christianity to lay a foundation for the spiritual life of man and for all his achievements in the knowledge of his own nature and in the realization of his true relation to God.

CHAPTER X

Christian Community

THE CHARACTER OF PERSONALITY IS ONLY FULLY REVEALED IN fellowship, for personality is essentially social. It is because love is a constitutive element in personality that it transcends any limited individualism. Beginning in the profound sense of the freedom of the individual in thought and moral will, personality develops into the freedom also to love, and, indeed, discovers in itself the necessity to love. But love is a bond between persons. Therefore, the full meaning of personality is the transcendence of self and the creation of a society. The implication of Christian personality is community of life, the fellowship of the saints, the Kingdom of God.

It is a false antithesis, therefore, to set "personal" over against "social" in Christianity and to think of personal morality or personal salvation as opposed to social righteousness and social salvation. For the true polar opposite of "social" is not "personal" but "individual." Personality is as much one as it is the other. The basic needs of man are for freedom— that is the individual side of it; and for fellowship—that is the social side. Lacking either man is not a true person. There must be the exercise of individual freedom and responsibility, but there must also be the expression of oneness with other persons in a common life, if personality is to be true to its own nature. There is no such thing as purely individual virtue, for morality is always a matter of right relations between persons. Righteousness is rooted in the choice and decision of the individual but its field of application and realization is society.

There must be at least two persons if there is to be any moral goodness.

Now, this social-individual conception of personality underlies the whole enterprise of Christianity in history. As we have spoken of "Christian" truth, so we speak of "Christian" personality, and "Christian" community. Someone may ask, Why not simply say "true" personality and "true" community? Certainly we hold this conception of personality to be true and the only true conception. But we have to recognize that it has rivals and that there are other religious and secular philosophies of life which in some degree deny it. The forging of such an ideal has been a long process, as I have tried to suggest in the foregoing chapter. The personal-moral relation between man and God is not fully developed in any other religion and it is flatly contradicted by some. For example, Karma in Hinduism makes the moral life mechanical and even mathematical. Islam denies the freedom of man, thus destroying the moral character of religion, and makes man's relation to God less than personal. Buddhism does not believe in the reality of personality and seeks a way of escape from the illusion of individual existence. Judaism is still limited by the concept of a legal morality which makes it difficult for the full freedom of personality to assert itself. It must be admitted that historic Christianity has in large measure suppressed and misconstrued the personal-moral character of religion, and even at this late date it remains as a task still to be done to make even Christendom aware of the full implications both in religion and in ethics of its own conception. But it is the true conception of personality, and the practical task of Christianity in the world is to make it clear and to work for the full realization of its meaning.

The only direct, courageous, and fully developed expression of the meaning of true community is to be found in the teachings of Jesus. Jesus' great dream and idea is the Kingdom of God. His precepts and his parables and such commands as he laid upon his disciples define and describe it and make clear the conditions for its coming among men and for the entrance of any man into it. His ideal of individual character is really derived from his more inclusive conception of the new society which he called the Kingdom of God. Such a society cannot exist unless men are radically sincere, and so in the Sermon on the Mount he insists that goodness shall be a matter of motive and inner attitude as well as of outward action. It cannot exist unless individuals are freed from selfishness, so he insists that those who want to save their own lives shall lose them, while those who lose their lives "for my sake" shall find them. The conquest of self in Christianity, however, is not merely self-denial, either in the moral sense or, metaphysically, as a denial of the reality of the self. It is, on the contrary, denial of the limited individual self in order that the larger self may be achieved in fellowship with others. It is an affirmation of the social character of the self or of personality. The achieving of these inner changes in the individual is always represented in Jesus' teachings as necessary for entrance into the Kingdom of God. "Except your righteousness shall exceed the righteousness of the scribes and pharisees you shall in no wise enter into the Kingdom of Heaven." They are never of importance for the individual taken apart from his fellows, as a means merely for some theoretical purification or perfection of his character or for gaining the approval of God and so insuring entrance into heaven. Jesus does not tell men how to get to heaven but he does make abundantly clear the conditions of entrance into the Kingdom of Heaven and of continued participation in its fellowship.

This social fellowship of the Kingdom is the great treasure, the supreme objective. To find it means life, to miss it means to be cast into the outer darkness. The parables of the Kingdom in the thirteenth chapter of Matthew should be put alongside the Sermon on the Mount. If the latter makes plain the character of the Kingdom and the way one qualifies for entrance into it, the former express Jesus' sense of its ultimate value as the final end and meaning of human existence. Jesus' first use of the term "gospel" reveals two things; first, the primacy of the Kingdom; and second, the demand upon each man to prepare himself for it: "Now after John was delivered up, Jesus came into Galilee, preaching the gospel of God, and saying, The time is fulfilled and the Kingdom of God is at hand: repent ye and believe in the gospel."[1] The "gospel," then, or the "good news," is the announcement of the imminent coming of the Kingdom of God. The original meaning of "gospel" is social; the "social gospel" is prior to the gospel of individual regeneration or salvation, because the change of the individual upon which Jesus insists is a change which the realization of this new community demands. "Repent and believe this good news," is the call for each one to change his inner motives and attitudes so that he may have a part in the Kingdom which is at hand.

Thus, while the social ideal of the Kingdom of Heaven was the great objective in the mind of Jesus, his approach to its realization was through a change in the individual. He proposed no program of social, political or economic change. He

[1] Mark 1:14, 15.

did not discuss the issues and principles of an external order
of human society, although he certainly expected a completely
new order. Whether he shared the apocalyptic expectation
of his time and believed that God would come to destroy
the old world and create a new one is not certain. There are
many references in his words to such a final catastrophe as a
prelude to the new heaven and the new earth. But there are
also many things that suggest that he really put his confidence in the quiet and slow outworking of the spirit and
truth which he communicated to his disciples. The Kingdom
of Heaven is like leaven which is hidden in the lump and
which secretly works until the whole lump is leavened. His
disciples are the salt of the earth and the light of the world.
This much is certain, that if men follow the teaching and
example of Jesus himself they will fit into a scheme of quiet
growth and inner transformation of society by peaceful means
rather than into any plan of violent change. It is true that
the apocalyptic miracle was not thought of as a human act or
as requiring the cooperation of men. It seems to represent
Jesus' feeling of the futility of all human efforts really to
change the total scheme of life and the conviction that God
Himself must come into the picture and violently and ar-
bitrarily create a new order. That Jesus was fully aware of
the vast forces of human selfishness arrayed against his ideal
seems clear and that he anticipated divine wrath upon the
ways of men and violent revolutions among men before the
ideal was realized is also evident. Whether this is thought
of as summed up in one great cosmic catastrophe directly
managed by God, or conceived as the violent aspect of the
long human struggle in which evil finally destroys itself and
the persistent vitality of good will wins the earth for the

meek, at any rate violence has no part in the course laid out for those who seek entrance into the Kingdom by repentance, by inner purity, by self denial, by forgiveness and loving service. The first responsibility of the Christian for the coming of the Kingdom has to do with the moral renewal of his own life. Since personality is social as well as individual, however, this change of the individual person is a change in the character of his relation to all other persons. The new person seeks with others of like spirit a new social bond, a new society. No new social order is possible without this new man to constitute it, but the new man cannot exist without working for a new social order.

The new fellowship cannot be maintained in the world without changing the outer form of society. That much is implied even in the apocalyptic view of history. The Christian community is constrained by the law of its own inner life to seek concrete embodiment of its ideal in the common life. Such spiritual compulsion is more urgent and authoritative and more thorough-going than any definitely drawn program for the reordering of human society in economics, politics, or even in morality. The difference is that between the absolute and the relative. The law of the inner life of the Christian is an absolute law, the law of love; the authority of any specific order of society is relative and temporary.

This declaration that love is the absolute law of the Kingdom of God, calls for a further word regarding the Christian meaning of the term. There is a world of difference between the selfish desire that is often meant by love, a desire which seeks self-indulgent satisfaction; and the self-giving and self-forgetting love which is fulfilled in a life of fellowship and service. To indicate this latter passion we often use the term "good will," because it is an impulse to good action. But "love" is the richer term if rightly understood, for the will is moved by some kind of emotion and love is primarily a desire for the good of others. The will that is good is good not because it obeys a command, even a command of God, but because it is determined by love. After all, the royal law, the divine law *is* love, as the New Testament says in many ways. That gives a new meaning to "law," and makes it not the mandate of another will, nor a compulsion of the natural order of things, but the reign of one's own heart over the will. When will obeys love, then and only then is it good. One might translate this into our contemporary speech and point out that the pure heart, the heart that loves, is the heart of the fully socialized person, that is, of the person who loves all others, even his enemies. This is the absolute in the moral life, the absolute rightness and authority of love. Every specific act is relatively good; it may be good at one time and bad at another, depending upon conditions. But it is always right to love and never right to hate one's neighbor. It cannot be claimed that any particular Christian always fulfills this law, but that is a matter of the imperfection of the individual and not a defect in the law itself. It is the basis of Jesus' lordship over men that he did love even his enemies and asked forgiveness for those who slew him.

The political state, the civil laws, the economic order, the social practices of men are all relative. One is better than another at any given time, but none is either absolutely good or absolutely bad. It is in this field of relative values, however, that the Christian must work toward the realization in time of the Kingdom of God. So long as men expected God to change the whole face of things by a cosmic revolution there was no call for such human effort. But two millenniums have passed and it seems now quite apparent that this is a task for men. It is true that there still remains, in a large part of the Church, the conviction that the world is hopelessly lost and that man cannot do anything to help himself. Religion for many is still centered upon the life after death; final escape from this life rather than its redemption constitutes for them the end of religious devotion. But over against this attitude we must place the persistent this-worldliness of Jesus, his "gospel" of the coming of the Kingdom, and his prayer "Thy Kingdom come, on earth as it is in heaven." I shall not argue the matter here, however. Most of the people who read this book will be those who are interested in the practical tasks involved in the realization of the Kingdom of God in the earth. And my whole thesis that Christianity furnishes an adequate working faith for the world assumes that God seeks to embody His purpose in history and to create a community of men of good will upon the earth. If this assumption is not sound, then it is nonsense to look to Christianity for a working faith; we might just as well leave to the communist or the fascist, or the Moslem, the practical job of ordering human life upon the earth.

But how is the Christian to work for the realization of the Kingdom of God if there is no pattern of human society that is Christian and no program of action that can claim the full authority of Christ? This question is partly the challenge of a deeply serious desire to be Christian in deed and in truth; it is partly the demand of impatience and a misconception of the nature of the Kingdom of God. For the making of patterns and the formulating of programs is always a task for the intelligence and good will of Christian men. There is no pattern laid up in heaven. There is a Purpose and even, taken in a very large sense, principles which can claim the absoluteness of the divine in human conduct. But patterns and programs are always directed toward the specific needs of particular people and particular times. This is the realm of human freedom and responsibility.

The Church has not always realized this distinction. There are two ways in which religion has tried to claim for some specific form of conduct the absolute authority of God. One is by the development of a legal system such as was found in Judaism and such as Islam still tries to enforce. Medieval Christianity took the same course. The other is to claim "guidance" for the details of daily conduct so that one has all the authority of the eternal God for the choice one makes in very trivial things. Both ways are based on a misconception of the place of God's will and therefore of the absolute in personal and social morality. And they also renounce the responsibility of man himself to assume the task of constructing plans of action and to express as best he may in the conditions of the time and place the meaning of goodness. Those plans are relative; even if a course of action should perfectly express Christian good will today, the ceaseless change that life brings might well mean that tomorrow it would thwart good will. "New occasions teach new duties, time makes ancient good uncouth, etc." Human action is human, both in its thought pattern and in its execution. The great fallacy has been the belief that a thought pattern could be found which could be identified with the will of God. Whenever that has been taken seriously and organized into a religio-political scheme of life, conduct has become fixed into moulds. Then the changes which life inevitably brings have been covered up by elaborate casuistry, which is an attempt to change the pattern while claiming that it is not really changed. Judaism, Islam, and Medieval Christianity all built such top-heavy structures of this kind that they tumbled of their own weight.

But God does set certain great objectives before men and His purpose is the will that they be realized. These are the objectives of Christianity, and I have defined them as Christian truth, Christian personality, and now Christian community. It is certainly the will of God that all men shall come to a knowledge of the truth, especially the truth revealed and embodied in Christ. It is certainly the will of God that all men shall become like Christ in personal character. It is certainly the will of God that His Kingdom shall come on earth as in heaven. These objectives are all clearly Christian and they are so bound up with one another that they are really one. They represent the broad outlines of the purpose of God for man. That purpose is the absolute with which we have to do. All plans and efforts to realize it in our human life must be the product of men whose hearts and wills are devoted to the purpose. The relative, changing form of those patterns of conduct does not detract from the absolute and unchanging purpose of God which we are seeking to serve.

We may characterize that purpose in general as the honoring and making honorable of human personality. There are Christian thinkers today who will take exception to this; it seems to make man too important. Dr. H. Kraemer, for example, says "I believe that in the atmosphere of the Gospel we cannot speak of the 'sanctity of human personality.' This is a modern conception, wrongly derived from the Bible and compounded with the right idea that man, being God's creation, has as such a God-given greatness." He says also: "In the Gospel all interest revolves around man as a prodigal son: lost, but an object of God's redeeming love. All attention is concentrated on God's searching love, not on a postulated value or dignity of man."[2] It is certain that in the gospel man is always conceived as deriving his worth and dignity from the fact that he is created in the image of God and that he is the object of God's love. He has no sacredness or value apart from God. But the "sanctity of human personality," while the phrase may be modern, is just as certainly a conception, not modern, but first clearly expounded in the New Testament. Else what did Jesus mean when he said "The Sabbath was made for man and not man for the Sabbath. . . . Are not two sparrows sold for a farthing; you are of more value than many sparrows; the very hairs of your head are all numbered. . . . How much, then, is a man of more value than a sheep? . . . What shall it profit a man if he gain the whole world and lose his own life, or what shall a man give in exchange for his life?" Ministry to the hunger and other human needs of men out of human sympathy was claimed by Christ as ministry to himself. No such value has ever been placed upon man, no such claim to the sacredness of human personality as that attributed to it by Jesus. We do not err nor go astray from the clear revelation of God's purpose in the Gospel when we accept as the great end to be achieved in human life the honoring and the making honorable of human personality. In this we are working with God and lending ourselves to Him as the agents of His will.

With this dominant ideal and purpose Christianity measures and judges all human institutions by its own criterion. Business, politics, education, recreation, art, religion must be

[2] The International Review of Missions, for October, 1937, p. 540.

judged in the light of it. No state or economic order, either capitalistic or communistic, has moral justification except as it serves to honor human personality and to make personality in all men honorable. Christianity does not concede the irresponsibility of any of these functions of organized society as regards the interests of personality. No political state is an absolute, but exists to serve and promote the true welfare of men. Business can take refuge neither behind impersonal economic law nor the demands of profit. All special standards, professional and otherwise, are subordinate to the dominant standard of a Christian community which is the development of free persons and the fostering of a fellowship of men based on mutual regard and cooperation.

It is personality, both in its individual and social aspects, that is the great and sacred value to be served. The root of the evil in our common life is disregard of personality, but that disregard itself is rooted in the hearts of individual men. Systems consolidate and express the anti-personal and antisocial attitude, but only individual persons think and feel and will. The dishonor to personality can always be traced back to a wrong estimate of man and an immoral attitude toward man in the heart of individual men. However the individual may be conditioned and influenced by social and economic institutions, the *locus* of an anti-social will is in the individual, and there it must be dealt with if social organization and process are to be changed for the better. Jesus' appeal to the individual to repent and be converted is the true approach to the problem of social immorality. It is men with moral intelligence and courage sufficient to stand against evil social practices who furnish the power and the initiative to effect social reform. Despite all social conditioning and the limitations environment places upon men each individual has the ultimate power and freedom to protest and to make his own moral integrity before God and his will to have justice done among men the vantage point for a creative effort to make the common life more righteous. It is somewhat paradoxical but true that the social prophet, who is most keenly aware of the power of social environment to mould the character of individual men, is at the same time a living demonstration of the power of the individual to turn upon that environment the judgment of a free moral intelligence.

We do a great disservice to the cause of the Kingdom of God, therefore, when, even by implication we teach men that they are, morally, as well as in other ways, the hapless victims of social circumstance and that they are to be pitied only and not censured for their moral failures. Statistically it is true that character is quite largely formed by environment and that such an index as child delinquency is in pretty definite ratio to poverty and bad social surroundings. We need still to be told that; but we also need to tell every individual that there is within himself a capacity for moral freedom and the ultimate power to defy external conditions and to become, as many have been and are, creative centers for the redemption of an evil world. This is an affirmation of the basic character of personality; if one wants to use the term, this is Christian individualism. Its main feature is that it is not, like the economic individualism some today advocate, irresponsible toward society. On the contrary a sense of responsibility toward society and genuine devotion to social righteousness are the motives that sustain individual integrity against the pressure of social practice.

The social idealist who says that the root of social evil is in the capitalistic system overlooks this fact that the individual moral will is the only true seat of moral good or evil. One has only to read the Bible to discover social injustice, oppression, and exploitation existing in exaggerated form long before the rise of capitalism. There seems to be a tacit assumption in both Old and New Testaments that the rich man is a bad man. Even in the Psalms it is the poor man who is the true worshiper of Jehovah; the rich man is his enemy and oppressor. The prophets are filled with denunciation of the rich and powerful. There is a remarkable but unnoticed verse in the fifty-third chapter of Isaiah, famous for its portrait of the suffering servant of Jehovah: "And they made his grave with the wicked *and with a rich man* in his death." The New Testament abounds with sayings which bear out the conviction that riches are fatal to character and a source of social evil. "Where a man's treasure is, there will his heart be also." "It is harder for a rich man to enter into the Kingdom of Heaven than for a camel to go through the eye of a needle." The sole point of the parable of Dives and Lazarus is that the rich man, having enjoyed wealth and luxury in this life, was sent to hell when he died; and that the poor man, having suffered want on earth, was found in Abraham's bosom on the other side. Read the Epistle of James, especially the second and fifth chapters, and the account of the Sermon on the Mount in Luke for additional evidence that the Bible was written from the standpoint of the poor and humble and oppressed and that the common assumption is that the rich and powerful are enemies to their peace and chief sinners against God.

It is not, however, merely a matter of social injustice being charged to the rich. All religious leaders have looked upon wealth as one of the chief obstacles to the service of God and as tending almost irresistibly to the corruption of moral character. "The love of money is a root of all kinds of evil." "No man can serve two masters; either he will love the one and hate the other; or he will hold to the one and despise the other. You cannot serve God and mammon." Wealth ordinarily means self-indulgence and forgetfulness of God. It nearly always separates a man from his fellowman and quenches or limits human sympathy. Also, men quite commonly fight to defend their possessions; one main root of social as well as economic war is the determination of individuals and groups to keep what they have—and to get more. It is not, therefore, the capitalistic system but the selfishness of man and his natural impulse to gain possessions and to defend at all cost what he has that is the source of social evil. It is true that this impulse takes a highly organized and effective form in a capitalistic order, but it existed long before capitalism and it would be a rosy optimist indeed who would look for the disappearance of selfishness with the passing of capitalism. Christianity is not utopian; it has no confidence in the conquest of selfishness by any change of economic systems. But it does believe in the capacity of every man to respond to the grace of God with a change of heart and with the dedication of self to the social purpose of the Kingdom of God. Social justice must come and continue to come indefinitely, but the power by which it comes is the Spirit of God working in the hearts of individual men to deliver them from selfish individualism into the social consciousness which means salvation.

While the Christian purpose does not define a specific program and process, but leaves that to human intelligence and effort, Christianity does, nevertheless, require certain conditions for the attainment of its goal. From this vantage point it exerts an influence on social, economic, and political life. It has a stake in three basic conditions for the fulfilment of its central aim, which may be described as *intellectual liberty, democracy,* and *government by law.*

Intellectual liberty does not mean mental irresponsibility, nor the license to say anything we please. It does mean freedom to know the truth and to speak the truth. Freedom of thought and speech about all matters of vital importance to the life of man is the elemental form of respect and honor toward personality. If man is to be free, if he is to develop the powers which are latent in him, he must be accorded the right to use his own intelligence in knowing the world in which he lives, and the forces and conditions that determine his duty and his well-being.

There are many assaults upon this elementary right today. A characteristic of one-party government is its drastic repression of intellectual freedom. It allows no facts to be made known that are not favorable to the existing regime. History becomes largely myth and propaganda. In all countries under such government the teaching of history must be done by nationals, because it must be made to support the purposes and the ideology of the state. There are powerful groups in our own country that are trying to exercise similar suppression of knowledge and teaching in our schools and colleges. Unbiased investigation of the facts of our own history is condemned as "radical" and "dangerous" and "un-American." In the matter of religious freedom we have come to another era of limitation and practical prohibition in various parts of the world. Russia allows freedom of worship and freedom of anti-religious propaganda, but not freedom of religious teaching. Turkey also permits freedom of belief and worship but puts severe restrictions upon the teaching of any religion. Mexico has made it illegal for anyone but a citizen of Mexico to be a minister of religion and has substituted naturalistic theory for the teaching of religion in the schools. All countries require religious schools to submit their curricula for official approval. Much of this restriction is due to the misdeeds of organized religion in the past—the Orthodox Church in Russia, the Moslem power in Turkey, and the Roman Catholic hierarchy in Mexico—and a liberal Christian cannot but have much sympathy with the governments that have taken such drastic measures to free themselves from the evils of clericalism. It remains true, however, that freedom of religious teaching as well as of worship is required if the mind of man is to have ultimate access to the truth about God and know for himself the way that wins the free response of his heart and will.

There is a radical difference on this issue between the Catholic and the Protestant interpretation of Christianity which we cannot ignore. The Church of Rome does not recognize or admit the right of the individual to freedom of thought in matters religious; but this right constitutes one of the fundamental principles of the Protestant Reformation. These two differing points of view create a difference in attitude all along the line and affect not only religious life, but social and intellectual and political ideals as well. The Catholic Church has the essentially dogmatic conception of truth and faith. It holds that it has the truth in its authorized body of doctrine and that its official hierarchy is alone competent to teach and interpret that truth. Truth in religion is not to be discovered by free inquiry and thought; it is to be gotten by learning from the Church. Thus the Roman Church is, on principle, opposed to religious freedom, one of its chief objects of attack being "liberalism." In a Protestant country it demands religious freedom, that is, full freedom to teach and practice its own doctrine, but it does not admit that non-Catholics have any inherent right to a similar freedom. The argument for this one-sided attitude is this: Falsehood and error have no rights, but only truth; therefore, only the Catholic Church has a real right to teach its doctrine because only it has the full truth. No one has any right to teach anything contrary to the Catholic doctrine because any such teaching is false and, as such, has no rights at all. This argument is made in good faith by the Catholic but it is based upon the very assumption which Protestantism denies, namely, that the Catholic Church and specifically the Pope is the officially authorized medium of spiritual truth. It begs the whole question as to what the truth is; in its concern to keep the doctrine pure the Church of Rome denies to all unauthorized persons freedom to search for truth and to teach what they believe in religion.

The liberalism which the Catholic Church denounces and which is the essence of the Protestant position holds to the freedom of individual judgment in religious faith. Liberal Christianity also has a great concern for truth but it expresses that concern by demanding that no obstacles shall be placed in the way of any mind that seeks to know it. It believes in real religious freedom. That does not mean that error has rights equal to truth, or any rights at all. The Catholic argument on this point is pure sophistry. Neither truth nor error has rights; only persons have rights, and all persons have the right to search for truth and to teach what they believe to be true. The liberal mind is convinced that the only way that men can be protected from systematic delusion and deception by states and ecclesiastical bodies is by the free exercise of their own minds in knowing the facts about all matters of importance, and by the freedom to tell the truth when they have found it, or at least to present to the world the evidence upon which they base their allegations of truth.

Liberal Christianity holds consistently to the claim for freedom as one of the main conditions for the honoring and the making honorable of human personality. In this all-important matter the Church of Rome specifically and in principle denies the true character of Christianity. This is not a pleasant thing to say and many Catholics are not aware that it is true, but it throws a responsibility upon all liberal Christian groups to work for freedom of thought without which the goal of Christianity cannot be attained.

Another condition for the attaining of the personal-social ends of Christianity is democracy. Democracy means freedom to act upon one's own apprehension of truth and right. Freedom to know without freedom to do is abortive, and democracy means freedom to do. It does not mean equalitarianism. All organized life must involve higher and lower positions, and that means authority and subordination. Organized society is always a hierarchy. A family is a hierarchy; a school, a hospital, a factory, and a municipality can exist and operate only as there are organization and authority and therefore inequalities of status. But this does not mean that each individual does not have basic rights and responsibilities. What democracy means is that the ultimate freedom and responsibility of the individual is recognized as the basis of society. It is difficult to get this principle fully expressed or operative in any human group. Those in authority, being human, do not always fully recognize the rights of the individual and, what is even more serious, the majority of individuals never assume the full responsibility, which democracy implies, of doing their own thinking and making their own moral decisions.

In this situation also we find a difference in principle between Catholicism and liberal Christianity. The Catholic Church does not trust the average man to govern himself; it is constitutionally sympathetic with monarchy. It assumes that men must be ruled, that, in politics as in religion, they do not know what is best for them and need a higher authority and wisdom to govern them. The ideal of political democracy and universal education is not Catholic but Protestant. However individual Catholics may value these things and may stand for social liberalism the official position of the Church of Rome today and the support it gives to the fascist powers reveal its essentially anti-democratic principle.

It must be admitted that the Catholic Church is more realistic than Protestantism in this respect, for the majority of men will not accept the responsibilities that go with democracy. But taking such a position in itself tends to discourage progress and the development of personal responsibility. On the other hand Protestantism is idealistic in its espousal of individual freedom and democracy; no people has ever fully risen to the challenge. But it is a challenge and a stimulus to the full realization of the capacities of personality and this idealism is truly Christian. Catholic Christianity points backward, Protestantism points forward, and the new world, the Christian community, lies in the future. The end of the road for Christianity is a society of free men under the reign of good will. It will be an essential democracy, not in the sense of equalitarianism, nor of the absence of authority and subordination which is anarchy, but an order of human life in which there has been written into the constitution of nations so far as law can do it the supremacy of personality above all institutional forms; and in which by tradition and education and habit there is accepted the principle that every man's conscience and mind shall be accorded freedom to know the truth and to do the will of God.

There is already implied in the foregoing a principle of civil government with which the fortunes of the Christian community are ultimately bound up, and that is government by law. In principle Christianity holds that all authority comes from God; its goal in human life is a theocracy, or the reign of God. Two ways to achieve this have been tried. The Catholic Church has held and still holds itself to be the specific channel through which that authority is mediated, believing that the civil state is dependent upon the Church for its authority, and ought to enforce the teachings of the Church. Protestantism, when it has tried to make the will of God effective in government, has done so by enacting laws mainly derived from the Old Testament, as was once the case in New England. The Catholic Church still maintains in theory its historic position although with little practical success. Orthodox Protestantism has given up long ago.

Liberal Christianity has an alternative to both these methods; its alternative is the original Christian idea and it gives a new lease of life and contemporary validity to the essential Christian doctrine of the reign of God. It makes no appeal either to Church or Bible as formal authority, but, claiming the rights and duties of democracy, it lays upon the heart of the individual Christian the task of using all the processes of social and political life in the interests of a Christian society. It affirms the necessity both of authority and of law, but claims that civil authority is vested ultimately in the people. The latter point is denied by the Catholic Church. Socially minded catholics make much of papal encyclicals on social justice, but this concern for social justice is no affirmation of democracy, nor acknowledgment that ultimate civil authority is vested in the people. So the papal power can, at one and the same time, support a dictator and preach social righteousness. It trusts to the principle of benevolent paternalism, which is its own principle in religion.

There are two general conceptions of government in the world. One is government by law; the other, personal government. The most conspicuous example of the latter just now is found in the reign of dictators. But it is no new thing in the history of the race; indeed it is older than the idea of constitutional law. In the Orient, generally, government has been personal; in the West we have a long tradition reaching back to the Greek city-state of government by law. It might seem that the former would be more consistent with the Christian ideal which makes personality supreme, but just the opposite is true. Lin Yu Tang complains of the lack in China of constitutional guarantees, because of which the common man suffers.[3] There, where personal government, under the Confucian ideal, reached perhaps its highest perfection, the individual man has had to depend upon the integrity, energy, and impartiality of the magistrate. Too often all three virtues have been lacking and the individual has had no basis for the assertion of his rights. Unless he has had a friend at court, or has been able to purchase the interest of the magistrate, his case

[3] Lin Yu Tang, *My Country and My People.*

has simply been ignored. There is a human touch in such personal government. Indians sometimes complain about British justice, not because it is not real justice but because it is so coldly impersonal. But Lin Yu Tang is right in his plea for constitutional guarantees. Government by law is *impartial* but it is not impersonal. It gives true honor to personality as such just because it disregards (in principle) all individual position and influence. This is the one basic equality that democracy claims—equality before the law. It is as far as human government can go toward realizing in principle the divine ideal. Even though the ideal of constitutional guarantees under government by law has never been fully realized, it has contributed immeasurably more to the dignity and worth and freedom of the individual than has the practice of personal government. The former is based on an essential equality, the latter on an essential superiority of the ruler over the ruled. The only way democracy can be made effective is through a government in which authority is derived ultimately from the people and in which elementary respect for personality is expressed in constitutional guarantees which honor man as man and which put the full power and integrity of government back of the humblest citizen's legitimate claims to rights and liberties.

The Christian community at which Christianity aims, while not identical with any political form or economic order, does therefore require these conditions for its realization. Means and ends are never separable in actual life. The means or conditions required for the Christian social-personal objective in history are intellectual liberty and democracy. Democracy, moreover, as truly conceived by Christianity, brings each man under ultimate moral responsibility to God. His value and

Christian idea of man and society. Those who must find a way that promises immediate victory will be discouraged with such a faith. But the ultimate ideal of a nation, the basic faith of man must be rooted more deeply in history and in God. All through history infinite enrichment has come into the lives of men in so far as individually and in fellowship they have devoted themselves to this ideal. It is a way for sober-minded men today, and for those who see realistically the vast evils of the common life, to follow and not be discouraged; it is the way of hope and ultimate victory.

Index